被自己所爱的人深爱着是什么样的感觉呢？会是什么样子呢？想要立刻回答的人，你要知道自己是多么幸福。

How it feels when you are loved by the one you love? How could it be like? If you want to answer it immediately, you shall know how happy you are.

# 世界上
# 最感人的书信

詹翠琴／编译

江苏人民出版社

**图书在版编目（CIP）数据**

世界上最感人的书信：英汉对照 / 詹翠琴编译 . —— 南京：江苏人民出版社，2016.1

ISBN 978-7-214-12911-6

Ⅰ . ①世… Ⅱ . ①詹… Ⅲ . ①英语－汉语－对照读物 ②书信集－世界 Ⅳ . ① H319.4：I

中国版本图书馆 CIP 数据核字（2015）第 315022 号

| | |
|---|---|
| 书　　　名 | 世界上最感人的书信：英汉对照 |
| 编　译　者 | 詹翠琴 |
| 责 任 编 辑 | 朱　超 |
| 装 帧 设 计 | 浪殿设计　飞　扬 |
| 版 式 设 计 | 张文艺 |
| 出 版 发 行 | 凤凰出版传媒股份有限公司 |
| | 江苏人民出版社 |
| 出版社地址 | 南京市湖南路1号A楼，邮编：210009 |
| 出版社网址 | http://www.jspph.com |
| | http://jsrmcbs.tmall.com |
| 经　　　销 | 凤凰出版传媒股份有限公司 |
| 印　　　刷 | 北京中印联印务有限公司 |
| 开　　　本 | 718毫米×1000毫米 1/16 |
| 印　　　张 | 11.5 |
| 字　　　数 | 148 千字 |
| 版　　　次 | 2016 年 5 月第 1 版　2016 年 5 月第 1 次印刷 |
| 标 准 书 号 | 978-7-214-12911-6 |
| 定　　　价 | 24.00元 |

*The Most Affecting Letters In the World*

# 世界上最感人的书信

世界上，有这样一种最幸福的约定，它浸润心灵的天，唤
醒生命的禅音。它带给我们温暖和力量，给予我们指引和希望，
让我们在多年后的某一天，收获一个完美而成功的人生。

## *A Mother'e Letter to the World*
## 一位母亲写给世界的信

Dear World,

My son starts school today. It's going to be strange and new to him for a while. And I wish you would sort of treat him gently.

You see, up to now, he's been king of the roost. He's been boss of the back yard. I have always been around to repair his wounds, and to soothe his feelings.

But now—things are going to be different.

This morning, he's going to walk down the front steps, wave his hand and start on his great adventure that will probably include wars and tragedy and sorrow. To live his life in the world he has to live in will require faith and love and courage.

So, World, I wish you would sort of take him by his young hand and teach him the things he will have to know. Teach him—but gently, if you can. Teach him that for every scoundrel, there is a hero; that for every crooked politician there is a dedicated leader; that for every enemy there is a friend. Teach him the wonders of books. Give him quiet time to ponder the eternal mystery of birds in the sky, bees in the sun, and flowers on the green hill. Teach him it is

亲爱的世界：

我的儿子今天开始上学。在一段时间内，他都会感到既陌生又新鲜。我希望你能对他温和一些。

你知道，直到现在，他一直都是家里的小皇帝，一直是后院的主人。我一直在他身边，为他料理伤口，给他感情上的慰藉。

可是现在——一切都将发生变化。

今天早晨，他将走下屋前的台阶，挥挥手，踏上他伟大的冒险征途，途中也许会有战斗、悲剧和伤痛。要在他必须生存的世界中生活需要信念、爱心和勇气。

所以，世界，我希望你握住他稚嫩的手，教他必须知道的一些事情。教他——但如果可能的话，温柔一些。教他知道，世界上有一个恶棍，就有一个英雄；有一个奸诈狡猾的政客，就有一个富有奉献精神的领袖；有一个敌人，就有一个朋友。教他感受书本的魅力。给他时间，去安静地思索自然界中永恒的神秘：空中的小鸟，阳光下的蜜蜂，青山上的花朵。教他知道，失败比欺骗要光荣得多。教他要坚信自己的思想，哪怕

far more honorable to fail than to cheat. Teach him to have faith in his own ideas, even if everyone else tells him they are wrong. Teach him to sell his brawn and brains to the highest bidder, but never to put a price on his heart and soul. Teach him to close his ears to a howling mob... and to stand and fight if he thinks he's right. Teach him gently, World, but don't coddle him, because only the test of fire makes fine steel.

This is a big order, World, but see what you can do. He's such a nice little fellow.

别人都予以否定。教他可把自己的体力和脑力以最高价出售，但绝对不要出卖自己的心灵和灵魂。教他对暴徒的嚎叫置若罔闻……并且在认为自己是对的时候站出来战斗。以温柔的方式教导他，世界，但不要溺爱他，因为只有烈火才能炼出真钢。

　　这是个很高的要求，世界，但请你尽力而为。他是一个多么可爱的孩子。

# 目 录 │ CONTENTS

Chapter 3 有一种温暖从未离开

世界上最感人的书信
The Most Moving Letters In the World

## Chapter 4

有一种交流受益一生

## Chapter 1

# 有一种甜蜜无处不在

*It is graceful grief and sweet sadness to think of you, but in my heart, there is a kind of soft warmth that can't be expressed with any choice of words.*

想你，是一种美丽的忧伤的甜蜜和惆怅，心里面，在我却是一种用任何语言也无法表达的温馨。美丽语录

# George Washington to His Wife
# 乔治·华盛顿致妻子

You may believe me, when I assure you in the most solemn manner that, so far from seeking this employment, I have used every effort in my power to avoid it, not only from my unwillingness to part with you and the family, but from a consciousness of its being a trust too great for my capacity; and I should enjoy more real happiness in one month with you at home that I have the most distant prospect of finding abroad; if my stay were to be seven times seven years. But as it has been a kind of destiny that has thrown me upon this service, I shall hope that has my undertaking it is designed to answer some good purpose...

I shall rely confidently on that Providence which has heretofore preserved and been bountiful to me, not doubting but that I shall return safe to you in the fall. I shall feel no pain from the toil or danger of the campaign; my unhappiness will flow from the uneasiness I know you will feel from being left alone. I therefore beg that you will summon your whole fortitude, and pass your times agreeably as possible. Nothing will give me so much sincere satisfaction as to hear this, and to hear it from your own pen.

George Washington

## 名人小课堂

乔治·华盛顿（George Washington, 1732 ~ 1799 年）

美国首任总统，美国独立战争大陆军总司令。1789 年当选，1793 年连任，后隐居。华盛顿被尊称为美国国父，学者们将他和亚伯拉罕·林肯并列为美国历史上最伟大的总统。

你可以相信我，我以最庄严的方式向你保证，我非但没有主动去谋求这个职位，反而是竭尽所能地推辞它。这不只是因为我不愿意离开你、离开家人，还因为我自知我的能力还不足以担此重任。此外，如果要我为了一个遥远的前程长年奔波在外，我倒宁愿在家与你一起享受哪怕一个月的真正的快乐。但是，既然命运之神选中了我来担当此职，我谨希望接受此任以实现崇高的目标……

我将充满信心地依赖上帝，迄今为止他一直在保佑我并赐福于我。毋庸置疑，这个秋天我一定会安然无恙地回到你的身边。我不会因为作战的艰苦和危险而感到痛苦。我的不快乐来自于我知道将你独自一人留在家，你会感到不安。因此，我乞求你鼓足勇气，尽可能愉快地度过你的时光。再也没有比听到你过得快乐更令我欣慰的了，再也没有比收到你的亲笔回信更令我感到满足的了。

乔治·华盛顿

## Nathaniel Hawthorne to His Wife
## 纳撒尼尔·霍桑致妻子

I do trust, my dearest, that you have been employing this bright day for both of us; for I have spent it in my dungeon and the only light that broke upon me was when I opened your letter. I am sometimes driven to wish that you and I could mount upon a cloud (as we used to fancy in those heavenly walks of ours). And be home quite out of sight and hearing of the world; for now all the people in the world seem to come between us. How happy were Adam and Eve! There was no third person to come between them, and all the infinity around them only seemed to press their hearts closer together. We love one another as well as there is no silent and love Garden of Eden for us. Will you sail away with me to discover some summer island? Do you not think that god has reserved one for us, ever since the beginning of the world? Foolish that I am to raise a question of it, since we have found such an Eden... such an island sacred to us two... whenever we have been together! Men we are the Adam and Eve of a virgin earth. Now, goodbye; for voices are babbling around me and I should not wonder if you were to hear the echo of them while you read this letter.

**名人·小课堂**

纳撒尼尔·霍桑（Nathaniel Hawthorne, 1804~1864 年）

19 世纪美国小说家，代表作《红字》已成为世界文学经典之一。霍桑是心理小说的开创者，擅长剖析人的"内心"。他的作品想象丰富、结构严谨。除了进行心理分析与描写外，他还擅长象征主义手法。霍桑对美国文学的发展做出了很大贡献。

　　我最最亲爱的妻子，我确信你早已为我们选定了今天这个晴朗的好日子；而我却一整天闷在城堡的主楼里，我唯一的一缕阳光是在打开你的信件后才得到的。我时常产生这样的愿望：我和你一同驾驭着一朵白云（就像我们过去曾经幻想我们在天堂里的漫步一样），远离世俗的喧嚣；到目前为止，似乎全世界的人都来妨碍我们。亚当和夏娃是多么幸福啊！他们之间就没有第三者介入，没有任何人骚扰他们，而他们周围无限的空间似乎把他们的心贴得更紧了。我们也如他们一样彼此相爱，却无法拥有一片只属于我们自己的静谧的爱的伊甸园。你愿与我一起远航，去寻觅夏之岛吗？你不认为上帝在创世记之初就为我们保留了这样一座岛屿吗？我提出这样的问题是多么愚蠢啊，因为我们已经找到了这样的伊甸园——属于你我两人的神圣的爱情岛……只要我们彼此在一起，我们就是那片净土上的亚当和夏娃。现在，我要和你说再见了，因为我的周围一片嘈杂。不知你展读此信时，耳边是否会有这些声音的回声萦绕。

# *John Adams to His Wife*
## 约翰·亚当斯致妻子

Prince Town New Jersey Aug. 28th, 1774

My Dr.,

I received your kind letter, at New York, and it is not easy for you to imagine the pleasure it has given me. I have not found a single opportunity to write since I left Boston, excepting by the post and I don't choose to write by that conveyance, for fear of foul play. But as we are now within forty-two miles of Philadelphia, I hope there to find some private hand by which I can convey this.

The particulars of our journey, I must reserve, to be communicated after my return. It would take a volume to describe the whole. It has been upon the whole an agreeable jaunt. We have had opportunities to see the world and to form acquaintances with the most eminent and famous men in the several colonies we have passed through. We have been treated with unbounded civility, complaisance, and respect.

We yesterday visited Nassau Hall College, and were politely treated by the scholars, tutors, professors and president, whom we are, this day to hear

**名人小课堂**

约翰·亚当斯（John Adams, 1735~1826 年）

美国第一任副总统，后来接替乔治·华盛顿成为美国第二任总统（1797~1801 年）。亚当斯也是由托马斯·杰斐逊组成的《独立宣言》起草委员会的成员，被美国人视为最重要的开国元勋之一，同华盛顿、杰斐逊和富兰克林齐名。他的长子约翰·昆西·亚当斯后当选为美国第六任总统。

我亲爱的：

我在纽约收到了你的来信，你很难想象得到它所带给我的快乐。自离开波士顿后，我连一次给你写信的机会都找不到，尽管信件可以通过邮寄信件这一方式，但是因为我害怕有人恶作剧，所以我不会选择那种传递方式给你写信。不过，现在我俩一共距离费城都不超过 42 英里，我希望在那儿私下找个专人为我们传递这封信。

我们旅程的细节必须保留到我回去后再与你分享，因为整个旅行经历丰富到都可以写成一本书了。总体来说，这是一次令人愉快的短途旅行。我们有机会看看世界，并有机会在我们路经的几个殖民地结识那些最杰出的知名人士。这里的人盛情款待了我们，并对我们表现出了极大的殷勤和尊重。

昨天我们参观了拿骚楼学院，并受到了学者们、导师们、教授们以及校长的礼遇，今天我们还要去听他们的演讲。明天我们将要去行动剧院。愿万能的上帝因对我们的高度信任，而赐予我们足够的智慧和美德。我们所到之处的人们精神似乎都非常良好。他们普遍地把我们的事业当作他们自己的事业来对待，并表示出坚定地遵守国会决定的决心。

preach. Tomorrow we reach the Theatre of Action. God almighty grant us wisdom and virtue sufficient for the high trust that is devolved upon us. The spirit of the people wherever we have been seems to be very favorable. They universally consider our cause as their own, and express the firmest resolution, to abide the determination of the Congress.

I am anxious for our perplexed, distressed province—hope they will be directed into the right path. Let me in treat you, my dear, to make yourself as easy and quiet as possible. Resignation to the will of heaven is our only resource in such dangerous times. Prudence and caution should be our guides; I have the strongest hopes, that we shall yet see a clearer sky, and better times.

Remember my tender love to my little Nabby. Tell her she must write me a letter and enclose it in the next you send. I am charmed with your amusement with our little Johnny. Tell him I am glad to hear he is so good a boy as to read to his Mamma, for her entertainment, and to keep himself out of the company of rude children. Tell him I hope to hear a good account of his accidence and nomenclature, when I return. Kiss my little Charley and Tommy for me. Tell them I shall be at home by November but how much sooner I know not.

Remember me to all enquiring friends—particularly to Uncle Quincy, your Papa and family, and Dr. Tufts and family. Mr. Thaxter, I hope, is a good companion, in your solitude. Tell him, if he devotes his soul and body to his books, I hope, notwithstanding the darkness of these days, he will not find them unprofitable sacrifices in future.

I have received three very obliging letters, from Tudor, Trumble, and Hill. They have cheered us, in our wanderings, and done us much service.

My compliments to Mr. Wibirt and Coll, Quincy, when you see them.

我为那些处于困惑和痛苦之中的人们感到忧虑——希望他们会被指引到正确的道路上。亲爱的，我希望你尽可能让自己拥有轻松和平静的心态。在这个危险的年代里，顺从上帝的意志是我们唯一的办法。谨慎小心是我们的指导方针。我最强烈的愿望就是：将来能看到一个更加晴朗的天空和更美好的时代。

请向我们的小纳比转达我温柔的爱意。告诉她一定要写信给我，并一起附在你下次寄给我的信里。我为你和我们的小约翰的逗乐而感到无比欣慰。告诉他，我很高兴听到他是一个乖巧懂事的好孩子，读书给妈妈听逗她开心，也没有与那些粗鲁的孩子为伍。告诉他，我希望当我回家的时候能看到他对词法和术语掌握得很好。代我亲吻我的小查里和汤米。告诉他们我应该11月份以前可以回家，但现在我还不知道到底多快能回。

请向所有问起我的朋友们问好——特别要向昆西叔叔、你的父亲及家人、塔夫茨博士及他的家人问好。我希望在你孤独时撒克斯特先生是一个好伴侣。告诉他，如果他将身心投入他的书中，尽管现在这些日子充满灰暗，我希望，他会发现他的付出在未来是不会白白牺牲毫无益处的。

我还收到另外三封非常亲切的问候信，它们分别来自图多尔、特鲁贝尔以及希尔。在我们的长途旅行中，他们激励了我们，并给予了我们莫大的帮助。

你见到威尔伯特先生、柯尔先生以及昆西先生时，请转达我对他们的问候。

你提到了雨，我倍感神清气爽。我希望我们的畜牧业得到了谨慎管理和细心经营。勤俭是我们的立足之本。这次旅行的花销将会很大——我们唯一的回报将是令人安慰的反思，即：我们为了公益事业辛劳工作、

Your account of the rain refreshed me. I hope our husbandry is prudently and industriously managed. Frugality must be our support. Our expenses, in this journey, will be very great—our only reward will be the consolatory reflection that we toil, spend our time, and tempt dangers for the public good—happy indeed, if we do any good!

The education of our children is never out of my mind. Train them to virtue, habituate them to industry, activity, and spirit. Make them consider every vice, as shameful and unmanly: fire them with ambition to be useful—make them disdain to be destitute of any useful, or ornamental knowledge or accomplishment. Fix their ambition upon great and solid objects, and their contempt upon little, frivolous, and useless ones. It is time, my dear, for you to begin to teach them French. Every decency, grace, and honesty should be inculcated upon them.

I have kept a few minutes by way of journal, which shall be your entertainment when I come home, but we have had so many persons and so various characters to converse with, and so many objects to view, that I have not been able to be so particular as I could wish—I am, with the tenderest affection and concern, your wandering.

John Adams

甘冒危险，并耗去了我们的时光——如果我们做了有益的事，那的确令人感到幸福！

我从未停止过思考孩子们的教育问题。培养他们良好的道德，使他们养成勤勉、活跃和富有进取精神的习惯；让他们把每一种缺点视为可耻和怯懦；激励他们要拥有成为有用之材的雄心壮志——使他们鄙视缺乏有用知识以及一事无成的人；把他们的抱负建立在伟大、坚定的目标之上，而蔑视那些细小、琐碎和无价值的事情。亲爱的，现在是你开始教他们法语的时候了。应该反复给他们灌输礼貌、优雅和诚实的知识，把这些美德牢牢地铭刻在他们的心中。

我以日记的方式记了一些备忘录，待我回家时可供你浏览消遣。不过，我们有那么多不同的人物要交谈，有那么多的事物要观察，所以不能够如我所希望的那样详细地叙述这一切——我带着最温柔的爱和关心，你的流浪者。

约·亚当斯

1774 年 8 月 28 日

写于新泽西普林斯镇

## *Mark Twain to His Wife*
## 马克·吐温致妻子

15 February 1869, Ohio

Livy, darling, how are you this morning? For it is morning, I guess, in as much as it is only half past 9, I have not got up yet. I only awoke a little while ago, naturally thought of you the first thing. I don't intend to get up till noon.

I wrote to our Mother,—if she will allow me to call her so—the letter is gone. If I had it back I would write it over again. I see that inletting the letter "write itself" it took entirely too unconventional a form. I forgot, occasionally, the fact that I was really writing to the PUBLIC, instead of to her. And so I elaborated what needed no elaboration, merely touched upon matters which should have been treated more fully. But don't you see?—if I had kept the public in my mind, the sense of being questioned cross questioned by outsiders, upon matters essentially private and personal, would have been so oppressive that I could not have written at all. It is hard to know that what you are writing (confessing) about your most delicate and private affairs is to be read by strangers and unlovingly criticized commented on at tea tables among miscellaneous groups who would often rather say a smart thing than a

名人小·课堂

马克·吐温（Mark Twain, 1835 ~ 1910 年）

美国的幽默大师、小说家、作家，也是著名演说家。他是19 世纪后期批判现实主义文学的优秀代表，代表作品有短篇小说《竞选州长》、《百万英镑》等，长篇小说《镀金时代》、《汤姆·索亚历险记》等。《哈克贝利·费恩历险记》是他最优秀的作品，曾被美国小说家海明威誉为是"第一部"真正的"美国文学"。

莉维，亲爱的，今天早上你好吗？因为现在是早上，我估计只有九点半左右，所以我还没有起床。我刚刚醒过来，自然而然地，我第一个想到的就是你。我打算赖到中午才起床。

我给我们的母亲写了一封信——如果她允许我这样称呼她的话——信已经寄出去了。如果我能把信收回，我会重写一遍。我知道，如让这封信"尽情演绎"，那么它将采取的完全是一种非传统的形式。我偶尔忘记了，我实际上不是给她而是给公众写信这一事实。所以我详细地阐述了那些本不该详细阐述的事情，却对那些应该详细阐述的事情一笔带过。但是你明白吗？——如果我把公众记在心上，那种被局外人询问或盘问纯属个人隐私的事情的感觉会是如此难以忍受，以至于使我根本无法写信。很难想象，你所写的（或承认的）关于你的最微妙和隐私的事情是怎样被陌生人阅读，又是怎样在茶余饭后被那些宁愿谈论精明的事也不想谈论一件好事的形形色色的人评头论足的。所以，我想，那也许毕竟

kind one. So I think that maybe, after all, there may have been a little natural impulse to holdback, instead of speaking out freely, though I was not really conscious of such an impulse. I do not think I am more sensitive than others would be under like circumstances.

I told Mrs. Fairbanks to have the ring made, and then express it to me at Elmira so that it would reach there about the 20th. And so you see I can put it on your finger myself, my precious little wife.

I wrote Twichell a short note yesterday to thank him for his kind efforts in forwarding our affairs. I told him we meant to lead a useful, unostentatious and earnest religious life, and that I should unite with the church as soon as I was settled, and that both of us, on these accounts, would prefer the quiet, moral atmosphere of Hartford to the driving, ambitious ways of Cleveland. I wanted him to understand that what we want is a home—we are done with the shows and vanities of life and are ready to enter upon its realities that we are tired of chasing its phantoms and shadows, and are ready to grasp its substance. At least I am—and "I" means both of us, and "both of us" means I of course—for are not we Twain one flesh?

I read a great deal in the Testament last night—why didn't we read the Testament more, instead of carrying loads of books into the drawing room which we never read? I thought of it Several times.

Clouding up again—well, is it never going to clear off? I will go to sleep again. Take this loving kiss and go to bed yourself, my idol.

Sam

只是一点点的本能冲动驱使我忍住，而不是毫无顾忌地畅所欲言，尽管我并非真正意识到这种冲动。在同样的情况下，我并不认为自己比其他人更为敏感。

我已经让费尔班克斯夫人去定做戒指，然后用快递寄到埃尔迈拉给我，那样我于 20 号左右就能收到。你看，这样我就可以亲手把它戴在你的手指上，我亲爱的娇妻。

我昨天给特威切尔写了一封短信，感谢他为促成我们的婚事所做出的种种努力。我告诉他，我们打算过一种有意义、朴素、真挚、虔诚的生活；等我一安顿下来，我就将与教堂联系；出于这些原因，我们俩都偏爱哈特福特的这种安宁、有道德的氛围，而不喜欢克利夫兰那种精力过剩、雄心勃勃的生活方式。我想要他明白，我们需要的是一个家——我们经历过生活的表演秀和浮华，准备迈进它的现实里——我们厌倦了追逐生活中的幻影，准备抓住它的实质。至少我是如此——这里的“我”是指我们俩，当然“我们俩”也是指我——因为我们俩不是成为一体了吗？

我昨天晚上读了许多《圣约》里的内容——为什么我们不能多读点《圣约》，却偏要把大量的从来都不看的书搬进休息室？我对这个问题想了好几次。

又是乌云密布了——唉！难道天空永远不会放晴吗？我还是去睡觉吧。接受我这充满爱意的吻，你自己也去睡吧，我的偶像。

萨姆

1869 年 2 月 15 日

写于俄亥俄州

# Winston Churchill to His Wife
## (Clementine Churchill)
# 温斯顿·丘吉尔致妻子
## （克莱门汀·丘吉尔）

My dearest one,

Alex and his aide-de-camp, who is the son of Lord Templemore, have left us after staying two nights. I hope Alex will come back again next weekend. He certainly enjoyed himself painting, and produced a very good picture considering it is the first time that he has handled a brush for six years. I have now four pictures, three of them large, in an advanced state, and I honestly think they are better than any I have painted so far. I gave Alex your message and he was very pleased.

The painting has been a great pleasure to me, and I have really forgotten all my vexations. It is a wonderful cure, because you really cannot think of anything else. This is Saturday, and it is a week since we started. We have had newspapers up till Wednesday. I have skimmed through them, and it certainly seems we are going to have a pretty hard time. I cannot feel the Government is doing enough about demobilization, still less about getting our trade on the move again. I do not know how we are ever to pay our debts, and it is even difficult to see how we shall pay our way. Even if we were all united

名人小课堂

温斯顿·丘吉尔（Winston Churchill, 1874 ～ 1965 年）

政治家、画家、演说家、作家以及记者，1953 年凭借作品《第二次世界大战回忆录》获得诺贝尔文学奖。他曾于 1940 ～ 1945 年及 1951 ～ 1955 年期间两度任英国首相，被认为是 20 世纪最重要的政治领袖之一，带领英国获得第二次世界大战的胜利。

我最亲爱的：

亚历克斯和他的副官坦普罗尔勋爵的儿子，在我们这里停留了两个晚上后就走了。我希望亚历克斯下周末还会再回来。他确实非常喜欢作画，而且还画了一幅很棒的作品，这是他操练了六年画笔以来，第一次画得如此好。现在的我熟谙画画之道，已经画了四幅画，其中有三幅大幅的。但是老实说，这几幅画是我迄今为止画得最好的作品了。我把你的消息告诉了亚历克斯，他听后非常高兴。

对于我来说，作画是一件非常令人高兴的事。作画时，我的一切烦恼都会被抛到九霄云外。作画真不愧为一个奇妙的疗法，因为此时的人们根本不会有其他杂念。今天是周六，我们出发至今已有一个星期了，可直到星期三我们才收到报纸。我粗略浏览了一下，看来我们真的将经历一段艰难的日子。我觉得政府在裁军方面的工作做得并不够，此外在重新促进贸易发展方面的工作也做得很少。我不知道我们怎样才能偿还债务；至于怎样才可不举债则更加有难度。即使我们全部团结在一起，组成一个联邦，集中起全国的所有力量，我们所面临的这个任务也是超

in a Coalition, gathering all the strength of the nation, our task might well is beyond our powers. However, all this seems already quite remote from me on this lovely lake, where nearly all the days are full of sunshine and the weather bright and cool.

Much better than the newspapers was your letter, with its amusing but rather macabre account of the journey to Wood Ford. I am longing to hear how our affairs are progressing. I do hope you are not overtaxing yourself with all the business that there is to do. We shall certainly not forget about Mary's birthday, but let me know what you have done about a present.

Considering how pleasant and delightful the days have been, I cannot say they have passed quickly. It seems quite a long time since I arrived, although every day has been full of interest and occupation. I have converted my enormous bathroom into a studio with makeshift easels, and there all this morning Alex and I tried to put the finishing touches on our pictures of yesterday. He has set his heart on buying a villa here on a promontory. I have not seen it inside, but from the outside it looks the most beautiful abode one can possibly imagine, and I understand that inside it is even more romantic, going back to the fifteenth century. He was a little startled when I pointed out to him that no one will be allowed to buy a foreign property across the exchange perhaps for many years.

He begged me to stay on here as long as I like, but I think I shall come back the 18th or 19th.I am doubtful whether I shall stop in Paris. I expect in another ten or eleven days I shall be very keen to get home again. Sarah has been a great joy, and gets on with everybody. She and I both drive the speed-boats. They are a wonderful way of getting about this lake, and far safer than

世界上最感人的书信
The Most Moving Letters In the World

出我们能力范围的，心有余而力不足。不过，这一切似乎已经离我很遥远，在这片美丽的湖上，几乎每天伴随我的都是明媚的阳光和凉爽宜人的气候。

你的来信里讲述的关于伍德福德既有趣又惊险的旅行故事可比报纸好看多了。我想听你讲讲我们的事情进展得如何。我真心希望你不要因为那些要做的事而让自己负担过重。我们当然不会忘记玛丽的生日；但是，请告诉我你准备了什么礼物呀。

就这些日子而言，真的令人非常惬意，但是我感觉时间还是过得很慢。尽管这里的每一天都充满乐趣，我过得也很充实，但是却依然感到来到这里似乎很长一段时间了。我把我的那间大浴室改装成了一个工作室，里面还摆着临时画架。今天整一上午亚历克斯和我都呆在那儿，努力完成昨天的画。亚历克斯下定决心要买下这儿的一幢海角别墅。我没有看过里面的陈设，但从外面看起来它确实是人们所能想象得出的最漂亮的住宅了。我知道室内甚至要更加浪漫，若是置身其中仿佛回到 15 世纪。但是，当我告诉他这里可能多年来一直不允许交易购买外国地产时，他颇感惊讶。

亚历克斯请求我继续待在这里，想留多久就留多久。但我想 18 或 19 号就回去。我还在犹豫途中是否在巴黎停留，但我多么希望再过 10 天或 11 天之后能回到我渴望已久的家。萨拉是我们的开心果，她和大家相处得很好。我们俩驾着快艇驰骋于湖上，感觉妙极了，而且比起意大利职业赛车手在连续弯路上全方位、全速驾驶小汽车或卡车可是安全得多。

the awful winding roads around which the Italians career with motorcars and Lorries at all sorts of speeds and angles.

Charles plays golf most days. There is a very pretty link here, and he has fierce contests with himself or against Ogier. His devoted care of me is deeply touching.

You maybe amused to see the elaborate form in which your telegram, which I rejoiced to receive today, was sent.

His dictation over, Churchill continued in his own handwriting:

My Darling I think a great deal of you and last night when I was driving the speed-boat back there came into my mind your singing to me "In the Gloaming" years ago. What a sweet song and tune and how beautifully you sang it in all its pathos. My heart thrills and I love to feel you near me in thought. I feel so tenderly towards you my darling and the more pleasant and agreeable the scenes and days, the more I wish you were here to share them and give me a kiss.

You see I have nearly forgotten how to write with a pen. Isn't awful my scribble?

Miss Layton has heard from her 'boy-friend' in S. Africa that she is to go out there (not Canada) immediately if possible to marry him. So she is very happy. Yesterday the South African officers came from their hotel and took her out to 'water-plane' behind their speed boat. She looked very handsome whirling along in the water and made three large circles in front of the villa before she tumbled in. Sarah is writing you now. The DB is starting.

Always your loving husband

查尔斯多数的日子都打高尔夫球。这里有一个很漂亮的高尔夫球场。有时他和自己打，有时与奥吉尔激烈对决。他对我悉心的照料让我感动万分。

我很高兴今天收到了你的电报，当你看到电文里精心制作的格式时，大概被逗笑了吧。

默写结束了，丘吉尔继续写他的信——

亲爱的，我对你是日思夜想。昨晚我驾着快艇返航时，我脑子里回想起你多年以前对我唱的一首歌，歌名叫做《在黄昏》。多么动听的歌曲！多么美妙的曲调！而且你唱得又是如此地哀婉动人！我的心在震颤，我打从心里喜欢你在我身边的感觉。亲爱的，我对你感到多么温柔啊！这里的风光愈是赏心悦目，日子愈是舒适惬意，我就愈发强烈地渴望你能来到我身边与我分享这一切，并给我一个吻。

你瞧，我几乎不知道怎么用笔写字了。我胡乱涂鸦的字迹是不是看着觉得很恐怖？

雷顿小姐收到了她"男朋友"从南非的来信。可能的话，她会立马动身去南非（不是加拿大）与他成婚，因此她高兴极了。昨天南非的官员们从他们的酒店过来，把她带到一架"水上飞机"上，那架飞机就停在他们的快艇后面。她在水上旋转着，在别墅的前方转了三个大圈才跌落下来，看起来真是酷毙了！萨拉现在也在给你写信。吃饭铃响了。

永远爱你的丈夫

## Clementine Churchill to Her Husband
### (Winston Churchill)

# 克莱门汀·丘吉尔致丈夫
## （温斯顿·丘吉尔）

My Darling,

I'm so distressed about the truss—I hope it is comfortable and does not worry you. Did you strain yourself or stretch unduly, and will you now be able to do your exercises which are so potent a preventative of indigestion? Please take great care of yourself.

I have big news. Mary is home from Germany for good and has applied for a position in London or nearby. It's very good of her because she was having a thrilling time in Germany. She asked to be sent home so that she could be near us. And they granted her request. She rang me up from Tilbury, and said 'I'm home for good'. I think she may be demobilized in February—I feel warmed and comforted by her presence.

I'm so happy to see from your letter that you are enjoying the beauty of the Lake sand the comfort and elegance of the Villa. I have had a most amusing letter from Sarah describing her apricot colored and mirrored bathroom.

亲爱的：

关于那个托带的事情，我感到非常苦恼——我希望它不会让你感到难受，也不会让你为此犯愁。你不要把托带绷得太紧，当然，也不要绷得太松，你现在还能运动吗？适当的运动能预防消化不良。请务必细心照顾好自己。

我有重大消息告诉你。玛丽已从德国回来再也不走了，并在伦敦或者是其附近谋了一份工作。这样对她很好，因为她在德国经历了一段令人不寒而栗的生活。她要求他们遣送她回国，那样她能和我们离得近了，他们也答应了她的请求。她从蒂尔伯里给我打来电话说："我要回家啦，而且永远不走了！"。我想她可能2月就可以回来了——想到她就要回来，我内心就感到温暖与安慰。

从你的来信中，我非常高兴看到你在享受着湖景的美丽风光以及别墅的舒适优雅。我还收到萨拉写来的一封有趣的信，她在信中描述了她那杏黄色的浴室，浴室里还装了镜子。

Work is progressing rather slowly, but I hope surely, on the Chartwell and London fronts—Whitbread is industrious and thorough and smiling. Max's hens are beautiful and have laid a few (a very few) eggs, of exquisite flavor but of diminutive size—about the size of a pigeon's egg. So we have to give two instead of one, to those who are registered with us. But Moppett says, they will get bigger and more numerous presently.

No German prisoners yet till after the Harvest. It will be lovely when the lake camouflage is gone and also the barbed wire.

Your Pal, Damaskinos is here being entertained by Mr. Attlee and Crankie. I see Anthony Eden attended the dinner.

I must hurry because your mail is just off. I'm sending 2 bottles of brandy as requested. I hope they are the right sort?

I enclose a cutting from the DT.

Yours loving

Clemmie

　　这里的工作进展相当缓慢，但我真的希望在查特维尔和伦敦前线的惠特布莱德勤勉、彻底并快乐地工作。马克斯家的母鸡很漂亮，到目前为止已经下了几个蛋了（仅有的几个），味道确实不错，但就是太小了——大概只有鸽子蛋那么大而已。因此，我们需要给那些跟我们登记过的人两个鸡蛋，一个不够。不过据莫皮特说，最近那些母鸡会产出更多且更大的鸡蛋。

　　丰收过后就看不到德国囚犯出来干活了。当湖上的掩饰物及铁丝网消失后，那周围将会变得非常美丽。

　　你的朋友，达马斯金诺斯在这里受到了艾德里和克兰基先生的款待；我见到安东尼·伊登也出席了晚宴。

　　你的信刚寄出，我必须快一点。我按你的要求寄去了两瓶白兰地，希望是你要的那种。

　　随信附上一篇来自《每日电讯报》的剪报。


　　　　　　　　　　　　　　　　　　　　爱你的克莱米

## Charles Dickens to His Wife
## 查尔斯·狄更斯致妻子

Tuesday morning, 15th April, 1851

My dearest Kate, —Now observe, you must read this letter very slowly and carefully. If you have hurried on thus far without quite understanding (apprehending some bad news) I rely on your turning back and reading again.

Little Dora, without being in the least pain, is suddenly stricken ill. There is nothing in her appearance but perfect rest—you would suppose her quietly asleep, but I am sure she is very ill, and I cannot encourage myself with much hope of her recovery. I do not (and why should I say I do to you, my dear?) I do not think her recovery at all likely.

I do not like to leave home, I can do no good here, but I think it right to stay. You will not like to be away, I know, and I cannot reconcile it to myself to keep you away. Forster, with his usual affection for us, comes down to bring you this letter and to bring you home, but I cannot close it without putting the strongest entreaty and injunction upon you to come with perfect composure—to remember what I have often told you, that we never can expect to be exempt, as to our many children, from the afflictions of other parents, mad that if—if when you come. I should even have to say to you, "Our little baby is

世界上最感人的书信
The Most Moving Letters In the World

026

## 名人·小课堂

查尔斯·狄更斯（Charles Dickens, 1812～1870年）

英国小说家。生于海军小职员家庭，只上过几年学，全靠刻苦自学和艰辛劳动成为知名作家。主要作品有《匹克威克外传》《雾都孤儿》《双城记》《远大前程》等，他是19世纪英国现实主义文学的主要代表。

我最亲爱的凯特，——现在请注意：你必须慢慢地仔细阅读这封信件。假如到目前为止你是匆匆读过，而未很好地理解（看出一些坏消息）的话，我指望你再从头看起。

小多拉突然病倒了，但她丝毫没有表现出一点疼痛的样子。她的脸上除了轻松安详，其余什么也没有——如果你见到她那模样，你会误以为她在静静地睡觉呢，但是我可以肯定她的病很严重，而且我对她的痊愈不敢抱太大的希望。我不认为（我为什么要跟你说我认为呢，亲爱的？），我完全不认为她有痊愈的可能。

我不喜欢离家外出，尽管我留在这里也无济于事，但我觉得我应该留在这儿。我知道你也不喜欢离开，让你离开我内心里也于心不忍。福斯特对我们还是像往常一样关心，他现在给你捎去这封信来并接你回家。不过，我在结束这封信之前，我不得不强烈地恳求和劝告你，回来时要完全保持镇静——记住我经常对你说的话：我们儿女多，其他父母们遭到的苦难，我们决不能心存侥幸自己能够豁免。假如——假如你回来的

dead," you are to do your duty to the rest, and to show yourself worthy of the great trust you hold in them.

If you will only read this steadily I have a perfect confidence in your doing what is right.

Ever affectionately,

Charles Dickens

时候，我甚至可能不得不对你说，"我们的小宝宝死了"，你仍然要对其他孩子尽到做母亲的职责，要向他们证明你自己值得他们对你的无限信赖。

　　只要你能冷静地读完这封信，我对你完全充满信心，你知道怎么做才是正确的。


　　　　　　　　　　　　　　　　　　永远的挚爱，

　　　　　　　　　　　　　　　　　　查尔斯·狄更斯

　　　　　　　　　　　　　　　　　　写于 1851 年 4 月 15 日

　　　　　　　　　　　　　　　　　　星期二早晨

# *Abigail Adams to Her Husband*

## 阿比盖尔·亚当斯致丈夫

Braintree August 19. 1774

The great distance between us, makes the time appear very long to me. It seems already a month since you left me. The great anxiety I feel for my country, for you and for our family renders the day tedious, and the night unpleasant. The rocks and quick sands appear upon every side. What course you can or will take is all wrapted in the bosom of futurity. Uncertainty and expectation leave the mind great scope. Did ever any kingdom or state regain their liberty, when once it was invaded without bloodshed? I cannot think of it without horror.

Yet we are told that all the misfortunes of Sparta were occasioned by their too great solicitude for present tranquility, and by an excessive love of peace they neglected the means of making it sure and lasting. They ought to have reflected says Polibius that as there is nothing more desirable, or advantageous than peace, when founded in justice and honor, so there is nothing more shameful and at the same time more pernicious when attained by bad measures, and purchased at the price of liberty.

I have received a most charming letter from our friend Mrs. Warren. She

名人小课堂

阿比盖尔·亚当斯夫人（Mrs. Abigail Adams, 1744 ~ 1818 年）

美国政界人物、女权运动先驱、书简作家，美国第二任总统约翰·亚当斯的夫人。她出生于马萨诸塞州的韦茅斯一颇具影响的殖民地政治家族。父亲威廉·史密斯为公会理事长，母亲伊丽莎白。有姊妹三人，排行老二。1764 年 10 月 25 日与约翰·亚当斯结为夫妇，此后，阿比盖尔便独自经营农场和操持家务，并担负起培养教育 5 个子女的责任。

你我之间遥远的距离让我感觉到，时间对我来说显得是那么漫长。自你离开我，差不多已有一个月了。我为我的祖国、为你、为我们的家庭感到无比忧虑，这种感觉使我白天过得沉闷，夜晚也过得不愉快。礁石和流沙到处都是。你能够或将要对未来采取什么样的方针路线完全还不得而知。不确定性和期望令人思绪万千。一旦受到侵略，有哪个王国或政府不必经历杀戮就可以重新获得自由呢？一想到这，我就不寒而栗。

然而，据我们所知，斯巴达的一切不幸缘于他们太渴望现在的安宁，缘于他们对和平的过分钟爱却忽略了那些保证国家持续和平的手段。他们应该思考波利比乌斯的话，基于正义与荣誉，没有什么东西是比和平更值得渴望或者更具有优势的；因此，再也没有比以卑劣的手段和以牺牲自由为代价来获取和平更令人感到耻辱、同时更致命的了。

我从我们的朋友沃沦太太那里收到了一封令人无比欣慰的信。她希

desires me to tell you that her best wishes attend you through your journey both as a friend and patriot—hopes you will have no uncommon difficulties to surmount or hostile movements to impede you—but if the Locrians should interrupt you, she hopes you will beware that no future annals may say you chose an ambitious Philip for your leader, who built up a monarchy on the ruins of the happy institution.

I have taken a very great fondness for reading Rollin's Ancient History since you left me. I am determined to go through with it if possible in these my days of solitude. I find great pleasure and entertainment from it, and I have persuaded Johnny to read me a page or two every day, and hope he will form his desire to oblige me entertain a fondness for it—we have had a charming rain which lasted 12 hours and has greatly revived the dying fruits of the earth.

I want much to hear from you. I long impatiently to have you upon the stage of action. The first of September or the month of September, perhaps may be of as much importance to Great Britain as the Ides of March were to Caesar. I wish you every public as well, as private blessing, and that wisdom which is profitable both for instruction and edification to conduct you in this difficult day—the little flock remember Papa, and kindly wish to see him. So does your most affectionate.

Abigail Adams

望我告诉你，她以一个朋友同时也是一个爱国者的身份，衷心祝愿你旅途顺利——希望你没有克服不了的困难，也没有带有敌意的运动阻碍你——但如果洛克里斯人阻挠你，她希望你要意识到未来的编年史不会说你选择了一个野心勃勃的菲利普人作为你们的领导，并在幸福制度的废墟上建立了君主制。

自你离开我后，我非常喜欢读罗林的《古代历史》一书，并决定假如可能的话，在我独处的这些日子里读完这本书。我从中得到了极大的快乐和消遣，而且我说服了约翰尼每天给我读一到两页，并希望他也能从满足我的愿望中形成他自己的读书欲望——我们这儿下了一场及时雨，连续下了 12 个小时，充分灌溉了大地上的果树，使其得以复苏。

我非常想收到你的来信。我迫不及待地想要知道你们的行动到达什么阶段了。对于英国来说，9 月的第一周或是整个 9 月，或许就像 3 月 15 日对于恺撒一样，具有重要意义。我祝愿你公事私事一切顺利，并希望那益于引导和启迪人的智慧在这困难的日子里为你指明前进的方向——小家伙们向他们的爸爸问好，并期盼着能见到他。你最挚爱的人也是一样。

阿比盖尔·亚当斯
1774 年 8 月 19 日
写于布伦特里

## Ludwig van Beethoven to His Immortal Beloved
## 贝多芬致 "永恒的爱人"

Evening, Monday, July 6

You are suffering, my dearest creature—only now have I learned that letters must be posted very early in the morning. Mondays, Thursdays—the only days on which the mail coach goes from here to K. You are suffering—ah! Wherever I am there you are also. I shall arrange affairs between us so that I shall live and live with you, what a life! Thus! Thus without you—pursued by the goodness of mankind hither and thither—which I as little try to deserve as I deserve it.

Humility of man toward man—it pains me—and when I consider myself in connection with the universe, what am I and what is he whom we call the greatest—and yet—herein lies the divine in man. I weep when I reflect that you will probably not receive the first intelligence from me until Saturday—much as you love me, I love you more—but do not ever conceal your thoughts from me—good night—as I am taking the baths I must go to bed. Oh, God! So near so far! Is our love not truly a celestial edifice—firm as Heaven's vault??

世界上最感人的书信
The Most Affecting Letters In the World

名人小课堂

　　路德维希·凡·贝多芬（Ludwig van Beethoven, 1770 ~ 1827年）

　　德国作曲家、音乐家、指挥家，维也纳古典乐派代表人物之一。他与海顿、莫扎特一起被后人称为"维也纳三杰"。他的代表作品主要有《英雄》、《命运》、《月光曲》等。贝多芬的音乐制作对音乐发展有着深远影响，他也因此被后世尊称为"乐圣"。

　　让你受苦了，我最亲爱的人儿——直到现在我才得知，邮件必须得在周一或周四早上很早的时候就寄出去——只有这些时间段才有从这儿到 K 城的邮车。让你受苦了——啊，无论我在哪儿，你都与我同在——为了生活，与你一起生活，我要安排好你我之间的事情。什么样的生活啊！就这样！就这样没有你在身边的日子——处处遭遇人性之良善的追击——我一点也不愿意这样。

　　一个人对另一个人的卑躬屈膝刺痛了我。当我把自己置身于浩瀚的宇宙时，我在思考自己是什么，而世人所称为伟人的又是什么——然而——这里蕴含着人类的神圣性。当我想到你也许要到周六才能收到我的第一封信时，我不禁潸然泪下——你深深地爱着我，而我对你的爱则更为浓厚——但在我的面前，请决不要把你的想法隐藏起来——晚安——我要去洗澡，然后必须去睡了。噢，上帝啊，我们距离这么近，却又相隔如此远！我们的爱情不是正像是一座天上宫殿——如苍穹一样坚固吗？

写于 7 月 6 日星期一晚上

## Chapter 2

# 有一种思念触动心扉

*Little compliments mean so much to me sometimes. Children have never been very good at listening to their elders, but they have never failed to imitate them.*

有时候，一点微不足道的肯定，对我却意义非凡。孩子们从来不会好好听从长辈的话，可是他们从来忘不了模仿长辈。

*E. B. White to His Mother*
*(Jessie Hart White)*
# 艾温·布鲁克斯·怀特致母亲
## （杰西·哈特·怀特）

Beta Theta Pi house

Ohio State University

Columbus, Ohio

26 April 1922

Dearest Mum,

I am hoping this will arrive on April 27 to greet you on your 42nd wedding anniversary, but I am a little late in starting it as usual. Your letter reached me at Mansfield, O. a couple of days ago where it was forwarded from East Aurora. I guess I told you in one of my previous letters that the way to reach me by mail is via 159 Park Place, East Aurora. Mr. Cushman does the forwarding.

So you've been gay for forty years

For forty years and two—

Been jolly all through smiles and tears

So you've been gay for forty years

> **名人小课堂**
>
> E・B・怀特（E.B.White, 1899 ~ 1985 年）
>
> 美国当代著名散文家、评论家，以散文闻名于世。他毕业于康奈尔大学，曾为多家杂志报社工作过。除了大量的随笔，怀特还写了三部童话，分别是《斯图尔特鼠小弟》（又译《精灵鼠小弟》）、《夏洛的网》、《天鹅的喇叭》（又译《吹小号的天鹅》），同样成为儿童与成人共同喜爱的文学经典。

最亲爱的妈妈：

我希望这封信可以在 4 月 27 日到达您手中，赶上庆贺您结婚 42 周年纪念日，但是如往常一样我的这封信写得有点迟了。您的信几天前在曼斯菲尔德到达了我手中，是从东奥罗拉那边转过来的。我猜想我在前几封信中的某一封信告诉过您，可以写信给东奥罗拉公园路 159 号的库什曼先生，让他转交给我。

四十年来您是如此快乐

四十二年了——

一路走来，充满着喜悦的微笑和泪水

四十年来您是如此快乐

一件多么少见的事情

我把我的爱寄送给您

四十年来您是如此快乐

四十二年了

我根本没想到，自从上周周一下午我们离开东奥罗拉后我竟会给您写信。我们在库什曼家停留到了复活节，还在罗伊克罗夫特家吃了复活

A thing one very seldom hears

I send my love to you

So you've been gay for forty years

For forty years and two

I hardly think I have written you since we left East Aurora a week ago Monday in the afternoon. We remained over Easter at the Cushman's and had Easter Sunday dinner at the Roy Croft's. The next day we left, clanking merrily out of town with our bed upon our back as goes the turtle...

Spring has arrived in Ohio. This is a flat state where red pigs graze in bright green fields and where farms are neat and prosperous—not like New York farms. We roll along through dozens of villages and cities whose names we never heard. They are typical of the Middle West. The oldest inhabitant is generally standing somewhere pulling a long white beard, the smithy door is generally open and the sound of the anvil to be heard, the village flapper is generally flapping up and down along Main Street in front of a group of jobless youths who help hold the drug store up, and somewhere there is always a housewife sweeping off a porch or carrying a spadeful of manure to the garden. Toward evening the country scenes become idyllic—the sort of thing you have seen in the moving pictures and never quite believed in. Sheep come drifting up long green lawns where poplars throw interminable shadows, come drifting up and stand like statues beneath white plum blossoms, while far down the lane and off in the fields a little Ford tractor moves like a snail across the furrows. Lilacs are in full bloom and the lavender iron-wood blossoms are coloring all the roads.

I've given up cigarettes until I get to California. Isn't that a good idea?

节晚餐。第二天我们就离开了，我们像乌龟一样，背上背着我们的铺盖，迈着欢快的步子走出了城……

俄亥俄州的春天已经来临了。这是一个平坦之州，红猪在翠绿的田野里悠闲地觅食。这里的农场非常整洁，呈现出一片繁荣景象——不像纽约的农场。我们的车轮一直向前滚动着，穿过了许许多多的村庄和城市，那些村庄和城市的名字我们从未听说过。这里是典型的中西部地区。最年长的村民通常站在某个地方，捋着长长的白色胡须；打铁铺的门通常是开着的，可以听到铁砧的声音；村里的年轻女子通常会沿着大街在一群没有工作的年轻人面前来回晃动着，那些年轻人通常都只是帮忙照看药店；在某个地方总有一个家庭主妇在扫着门廊，或者运满满的一锹肥料到花园去。接近黄昏时，乡村景色变得如田园诗一般美好——那是您只有在电影里才能见到的风光，您是不会相信的。羊群沿着长长的绿色的草地移动过来，白杨树在草地上投射下了冗长的阴影，羊群过来了，它们就像雕像一样站立在盛开的白梅树下。沿着远处的乡间小路望向田野，你可以看到一辆小福特拖拉机像一只蜗牛在阡陌间慢行。紫丁香花盛开，熏衣香铁树的花儿把每条路都装点得五彩缤纷。

我想在去加利弗尼亚前把烟戒了，我想这是一个不错的主意，库什也这么认为。同时我也很想尽快摆脱这些洁净的衬衫，现在穿着的已经是最后一件了。

福特牌汽车花销很惊人。自我们离开纽约到现在，维修费已花了75美分——50美分花在修理炸裂的散热器上，25美分则花在修理鼓风机皮带上。开支相当大。

纽约州是一个公路之州。这里有收费的公路，它一边是水泥路，另一边是泥土路。当你的车与另一辆车相遇时，假如你正好在水泥路这一边，那一切还好；但是如果你的车是在泥土路这一边，你要转到水泥路

Cush thinks it's great. I also am looking forward soon to giving up clean shirts. They're worse than cigarettes. I'm on my last one now.

The Ford is a tremendous expense. Repairs have cost up 75 cents since we left New York—50 cents for a busted radiator and 25 cents for a fan belt. Pretty heavy going.

New York is the state for roads. Here there are pikes, which are cement on one side and dirt on the other. When you meet another car if you are on the cement side all is well, and when you are on the dirt side you steer to one side, sink down indefinitely, and then get out and lift the car back onto the road again. That's why Fords can go places where heavier cars have difficulty. Whenever your Ford shows signs of weakening, you can lift it back where it belongs.

Tell Father he ought to read Benchley's Of All Things if he wants a good time. I read it the other day in Mansfield. It's about as funny as anything there is on the market today with the exception, of course, of the Cushman-White travelogues which are simply killing.

We'll be leaving for Kentucky on Friday morning. This place is so beautiful we want to stay for a day or so to become acquainted with it.

Congratulations again on your anniversary. Have a good time at Atlantic City honey mooning. Love to Father—tell him I received his letter and thank you. I mailed the slip to the Trust Company the other day in Mansfield.

Yours, Andy

上，说不定你的车就会陷下去。那样你就必须下车，然后把车拖回到路上。这就是为什么福特车能去的地方而重型车却存在困难，未必能去。无论什么时候福特车有抛锚的迹象，你能把它拖回到它原来的地方。

告诉父亲，如果他想拥有快乐的时光，那他应该读一下本奇利的《万花筒》。几天前我在曼斯菲尔德看过那本书。它几乎和当今市面上所有的其他东西一样有趣，当然库什曼·怀特的旅行见闻除外，那只不过可以拿来消磨时间而已。

我们星期五早晨准备动身前往肯塔基州。这个地方是如此美丽，我想再多呆一两天以加深对它的了解。

在您的结婚周年纪念日之际再次向您表示祝贺。祝愿您在大西洋城度过一个愉快的蜜月。代我向父亲大人问好——告诉他我已收到了他的信，谢谢您。几天前，我把那张便条寄到了曼斯菲尔德的信托公司。

您的：安迪

1922 年 4 月 26 日

写于俄亥俄州哥伦布

俄亥俄州大学

# T. E. Lawrence to His Mother（I）
## 托马斯·爱德华·劳伦斯致母亲（1）

Fleece Hotel Colchester

August 13, 1905

Dear Mother,

We came here from Ipswich over a rather hilly road 18 miles long. Still we took two hours over it; and walked about six hills; a proceeding Father does not like. We are feeding splendidly. Father is much better and has not coughed since Lynn.

I have had to give up Bures. We came by the other road because of the wind. Still I hope to get Pebmarsh tomorrow, and I got one rubbing yesterday so I'm not altogether mournful. I have sent off all my rubbings to Miss Powell.Hope she'll like them. I expect you have Will with you now. Will you please tell him not to let you do more work than is necessary to keep you in condition? Also tickle Arnie when he gets up and when he goes to bed all from me. Tell him there are dozens of butterflies fall sorts about here, some Red Admirals; and a lot of other very queer ones. Ask Beadle to come up here as he has never seen a Death's Head or some such insect. Norwich Museum he would have enjoyed. There was the largest collection of raptorial birds in

托马斯·爱德华·劳伦斯（T.E.Lawrence, 1888 ~ 1935 年）

英国军官，因在 1916 年至 1918 年的阿拉伯起义中作为英国联络官的角色而出名，被称为"阿拉伯的劳伦斯"。他的代表作品是《智慧的七柱》，许多阿拉伯人将他看成民间英雄，推动了他们从奥斯曼帝国和欧洲的统治中获得自由的理想。

亲爱的妈妈：

我们从伊普斯威奇郡到这里花了两个多小时，走过一条长 18 英里的山路，翻越了大约六座山。父亲不喜欢这样的行程。不过一路上我们吃得很好。父亲现在好多了，自从离开林恩以后他就再也没有咳嗽过。

我不得不放弃取道布尔斯。因为起风了，我们只好从另一条路走。但我依然希望明天能到达佩伯玛西。昨天我又得到了一块拓片，所以我不是那么悲伤。我已将所有的拓片寄给了鲍威尔小姐，希望她会喜欢。我想现在威尔正与您在一起。请告诉他不要让您过于操劳以免影响健康。此外，我不能在阿尼起床或上床睡觉时再去扰他了。告诉他这儿有很多不同种类的蝴蝶：如"赤蛱蝶"，以及其他一些很奇特的品种。也告诉比德尔，让他到这儿来，因为他还从未看过"骷髅天蛾"或诸如此类的昆虫。他肯定会喜欢诺威奇博物馆的。这儿收藏了最多的猛禽类标本，藏有现存 470 个品种中的 409 种。我在想如果他知道我没有去看那些鸟，而是去看了诺曼的 W.C.s 是否会惊恐得大叫。大厅里有一组令人恐怖的

existence 409 out of 470 species. I wonder if he'll shriek with horror when he hears that I did not look at them but went off and examined the Norman W.C.s. In the hall there was a thrilling stuffed group a boa constrictor strangling a tiger. We hope to return to Oxford Wednesday. Kindly take heaps of love from me for yourself. And when you've had enough, divide the remainder into three portions, and give them to the three worms you have with you. I wonder how the Doctor is enjoying Jerry. Don't forget the Canon's birthday next Sunday. We have had one post card from Will, one from yourself and one letter from you. Loud snores to all. Love to yourself.

Ned

蟒蛇勒死老虎的标本。我们希望星期三能返回牛津。请为您自己带上我无限的爱，并向您的三只小虫转达我的爱。我想知道医生到底有多么喜欢杰里。不要忘了下个星期天是坎农的生日。我们已收到了威尔的一张明信片，还有您的一张明信片以及一封信。向所有人大声问好！

爱您的：内德
1905 年 8 月 13 日
写于科尔切斯特
福利斯旅馆

# T. E. Lawrence to His Mother (Ⅱ)

# 托马斯·爱德华·劳伦斯致母亲（2）

Evreux

Sunday 11 August 1907

Dear Mother,

Father is out, and so I am at last writing to you. I would have written before, but was so busy taking photos, etc. at Chateau Gaillard. Beauvais was a wonderful place, and I left it with great regret for Gisors which was disappointing, (a large castle, but all the towers locked up), from Gisors we came to Petit Andelys. The Chateau Gaillard was so magnificent, and the post cards so abominable, that I stopped there an extra day. And I did nothing but photograph, from 6.a.m.to 7.p.m. I took ten altogether. And if all are successful, I will have a wonderful series. I will certainly have to start a book. Some of them were very difficult to take, and the whole day was very hard. I think Pt. Andelys would be a good place to stop at. The hotel is cheap, and very pleasant. The Seine runs near the back door. And the bathing is excellent, from a little wooded island in the centre of the river. There are plenty of hills within sight, and many interesting places. Also the scenery all along the river

亲爱的妈妈：

父亲出去了，我终于能给您写信了。我早就应该写的，但是一直忙于在盖拉德城堡拍照等等。博韦是一个迷人的地方，我带着无限的遗憾离开动身去日索尔（一个大城堡，但是那里所有的塔都被上了锁），这令我大失所望。我们又从日索尔出发前往小安德利斯。盖拉德城堡是如此富丽堂皇，然而那里的明信片却是那么的糟糕，以致使我在那儿多停留了一天。除了拍照，没做其他任何事，我一直从早晨6点拍到下午7点，一共拍了10卷。如果所拍的照片全部成功，我就有一套精彩绝伦的系列照了，那么我肯定得为此而写一本书。有些场景特别难拍，所以那一整天很辛苦。我认为小安德利斯是个不错的停留之地，旅店既便宜又舒适。塞纳河从旅店后门的不远处流过，在河中心的一个树林茂密的小岛有一个极佳的浴场。许多小山丘和有趣的景致尽收眼底。塞纳河沿岸的风光也非常优美。偶尔可以看到蒸汽拖船拖着一长串驳船从旅店门前驶过。整个地方被堆着城堡废墟的小山丘的阴影遮蔽着。我对你描述了这么多，

is exceedingly fine. Long strings of barges pulled by a steam-tug pass the hotel occasionally, and the whole place is overshadowed by the hills with the ruins of the Chateau. I have talked so much about this to you that you must know it all by heart, so I had better content myself with saying that its plan is marvelous, the execution wonderful, and the situation perfect. The whole construction bears the unmistakable stamp of genius. Richard I must have been a far greater man than we usually consider him. He must have been a great strategist and a great engineer, as well as a great man-at-arms.

想必你一定对它的情况心领神会了。那么，我最好满足一下自己的感觉，发表一下对盖拉德城堡的感慨。它的规划设计非凡，施工技艺精湛，选址位置完美。整个建筑物真是巧夺天工，实乃天才之作。理查德一世一定是一位远比我们通常所想象的还要伟大得多的人物：他一定是一位伟大的战略家，一位伟大的工程师，同时也一定是一位伟大的士兵。

于埃莆勒，星期日
1907 年 8 月 11 日

## Ernest Hemingway to His Mother
## (Grace Hall Hemingway)
## 欧内斯特·海明威致母亲
## （格雷斯·霍尔·海明威）

Gstaad, 5 February 1927

Dear Mother,

Thank you very much for sending me the catalogue of the Marshal Field exhibit with the reproduction of your painting of the Blacksmith Shop in it. It looks very lovely and I should have liked to see the original.

I did not answer when you wrote about the Sun etc. book as I could not help being angry and it is very foolish to write angry letters??and more than foolish to do so to one's mother. It is quite natural for you not to like the book and I regret your reading any book that causes you pain or disgust.

On the other hand I am in no way ashamed of the book, except in as I may have failed in accurately portraying the people I wrote of, or in making them really come alive to the reader. I am sure the book is unpleasant. But it is not all unpleasant and I am sure is no more unpleasant than the real inner lives of some of our best Oak Park families. You must remember that in such a book all the worst of the people's lives is displayed while at home there is a very lovely

欧内斯特·海明威（Ernest Hemingway, 1899 ~ 1961 年）

美国小说家。海明威出生于美国伊利诺伊州芝加哥市郊区的奥克帕克，代表作品有《老人与海》《太阳照样升起》《永别了，武器》《丧钟为谁而鸣》等，他凭借《老人与海》获得1953 年普利策奖及 1954 年诺贝尔文学奖。1961 年，蜚声世界文坛的海明威用自己的猎枪结束了自己的生命。

亲爱的母亲：

十分感谢您给我寄来马歇尔·菲尔德展览的目录，以及您在展览中展出的油画《铁匠铺》的复制品。这幅画看起来非常可爱，我真想看一看原作。

您之前的来信中谈到《太阳照样升起》这本书，我没有回信，因为我无法抑制自己愤怒的心情。写一封字里行间流露出愤怒心情的信是愚蠢的；而且，给自己的母亲写这样的信则远远不止愚蠢那么简单了。您不喜欢这本书那是相当自然的，我为让您读到引起您痛苦和厌恶的书而感到抱歉。

另一方面，我无论怎样也不会为这本书感到惭愧，当然在某些方面除外——例如，我可能没能准确地描绘我书中所写的人物，或没能将那些人物栩栩如生地展现在读者面前。我肯定这本书里的内容会令人感到厌恶。但这本书并不是所有的内容都令人感到厌恶；而且我肯定，它不会比我们最好的奥克·帕克家族真正的内部生活更令人感到厌恶。您一

side for the public and the sort of thing of which I have had some experience in observing behind closed doors. Besides you, as an artist, know that a writer shouldn't be forced to defend his choice of a subject but should be criticized on how he has treated that subject. The people I wrote of were certainly burned out, hollow and smashed—and that is the way I have attempted to show them. I am only ashamed of the book in whatever way it fails to really give the people I wished to present. I have a long life to write other books and the subjects will not always be the same—except as they will all, I hope, be human beings.

And if the good ladies of the book study club under the guidance of Miss Fanny Butcher, who is not an intelligent reviewer—I would have felt very silly had she praised the book—agree unanimously that I am prostituting a great talent etc. for the lowest ends—why the good ladies are talking about something of which they know nothing and saying very foolish things.

As for Hadley, Bumby and myself—although Hadley and I have not been living in the same house for some time (we have lived apart since last Sept. and by now Hadley may have divorced me) we are the very best of friends. She and Bumby are both well, healthy and happy and all the profits and royalties of The Sun Also Rises, by my order, are being paid directly to Hadley, both from America and England. The book has gone into, by the last ads I saw in January, 5 printings (15000) copies, and is still going strongly. It is published in England in the spring under the title of Fiesta. Hadley is coming to America in the spring so you can see Bumby on the profits of Sun Also Rises. I am not taking one cent of the royalties, which are already running into several thousand dollars, have been drinking nothing but my usual wine or beer with meals, have been leading a very monastic life and trying to write as well as I am able.

定记得，在这本书里，人们生活中所有最阴暗的一面都被揭露出来，但同时它还向公众展现了家庭生活美好的一面，以及我暗中亲眼观察到的那类事情。此外，作为一位艺术家，您知道一个作者不应被迫去为他所选的主题辩护，而应当接受别人对他如何对待这一主题方面的评论。我所描绘的人物肯定是心力交瘁、空洞虚伪和支离破碎的——而那正是我试图表达的。我只是遗憾在这本书里，我没能把自己真正想要表达给读者知道的内容写出来。不过，我的一生还很长，我有足够的时间来写其他的书，而且我所选的主题也不会总是一样——除了如我希望的，它们都将是关于人类的话题之外。

假如"读书俱乐部"的淑女们，在并不聪明的书评者范妮·布彻小姐的指导下——要是得到她对这本书的表扬，我倒会感到非常可笑——全体一致同意我为那最坏的结局而践踏天资等等——为什么那些淑女们要去谈论她们一窍不通的东西，还净说些蠢话呢？

至于哈德利、邦比和我自己——尽管哈德利和我已经有一段时间没有一同居住在同一所房子里（我们从去年九月份开始分居，到目前为止哈德利可能已跟我离了婚了），但我们还是最要好的朋友。她和邦比都很好，身体健康且生活愉快。按照我的要求，《太阳照样升起》这部书的所有收益和版税都会从美国和英国直接汇给哈德利。我从1月份最后一次看到的广告中得知，这部书已经第五次印刷（15000本），并且销量仍在急剧上升。这部书春季在英国出版，书名为《节日》。这个春天，哈德利将会到美国来，到时您就可以看到邦比得到《太阳照样升起》这部书的收益。版税共计已有几千美元，不过我一分钱也没拿。一直以来，我吃

We have different ideas about what constitutes good writing—that is simply a fundamental disagreement—but you really are deceiving yourself if you allow any Fanny Butchers to tell you that I am pandering to sensation-alism etc. I get letters from Vanity Fair, Cosmopolitan etc. asking me for stories, articles, and serials, but am publishing nothing for six months or a year (a few stories sold to Scribner's the end of last year and one funny article out) because I know that now is a very crucial time and that it is much more important for me to write in tranquility, trying to write as well as I can, with no eye on any market, nor any thought of what the stuff will bring, or even if it can ever be published—than to fall into the money making trap which handles American writers like the corn husking machine handled my noted relative's thumb .

I'm sending this letter to both of you because I know you have been worried about me and I am always sorry to cause you worry. But you must not do that—because, although my life may smashup in different ways, I will always do all that I can for the people I love (I don't write home a lot because I haven't time and because, writing, I find it very hard to write letters and have to restrict correspondence to the letters I have to write—and my real friends know that I am just as fond of them whether I write or not) that I have never been a drunk nor even a steady drinker (You will hear legends that I am— they are tacked on everyone that ever wrote about people who drink) and that all I want is tranquility and a chance to write. You may never like anything I write—and then suddenly you might like something very much. But you must believe that I am sincere in what I write. Dad has been very loyal and while you, mother, have not been loyal at all I absolutely understand that it is because you believed you owed it to yourself to correct me in a path which seemed to

饭时除了喝一点平时喝的葡萄酒或啤酒外，什么也没喝；我一直过着修道士般清贫的生活，并尽我所能地写出优秀作品。对于什么是优秀作品，我们有不同的见解——那仅仅是一种基本的不一致——但是如果您让范妮·布彻这类人告诉您，说我在哗众取宠之类的话，那么您就真的是在欺骗自己。我收到《名利场》《世界主义者》等刊物来信要我为其写短篇小说、文章、以及连载小说，但我最近6个月或者说这一年都没有发表任何作品（去年年底卖过几个短篇小说和一篇滑稽文章给斯克里布纳出版社），因为我知道现在是非常关键的时刻，对我来说，安心地写作并尽我所能地写得更好，既不去关注市场，也不去考虑写作能带来什么，甚至不去在乎我的作品能否出版——这些事情比掉入操纵美国作家们的赚钱陷阱重要得多，这个陷阱就像玉米脱壳机解决了我那著名的亲戚的拇指一样。

我知道您二老一直担心着我，所以我把这封信寄给您们，我很抱歉，让您们担心了。但您们不必那样做——因为，尽管我的人生可能遭遇不同的灾难，但我会永远为我所爱的人们去做我所能做的一切事情（我没有给家里写很多的信，因为我没有时间，也因为写信本身，我发觉写信是很难的一件事，因此只写那些不得不写的信——而且，我的那些真正的朋友都知道，不管我是否给他们写信，我都一如既往地爱着他们），我从来不是一个酒鬼，也很少喝酒（你们会听到关于我是酒鬼的传闻——人们总是把任何一个描写酒徒的作家冠上酗酒的罪名），而我所想要的只不过是安宁的环境和一个写作的机会。也许您们从未喜欢过我写的任何作品——您们也可能会突然非常喜欢某部作品。但是您们一定要相信，

you disastrous.

So maybe we can drop that all. I am sure that, in the course of my life, you will find much cause to feel that I have disgraced you if you believe everything you hear. On the other hand with a little shot of loyalty as an anesthetic you may be able to get through all my obvious disreputability and find, in the end, that I have not disgraced you at all.

Anyhow, best love to you both,

Ernie

我对于自己所写的东西都是非常真诚的。父亲一直是非常诚心的，而您，母亲，一点儿都不诚心，我完全理解这是因为在您看来，我走的是一条灾难性的道路，而您认为您有义务来纠正我。

因此，或许我们该停止那一切了。我敢肯定，在我的人生道路上，假如您相信道听途说的每一件事，您将会找到很多的理由觉得我让您蒙羞了。但在另一方面，如果您带有一点点儿诚心作为麻醉剂，您也许会明白，我所有显而易见的声名狼藉，到最后发现事实上我一点儿都没有让您蒙羞。

不论怎样，真心的爱献给您二老。

欧 尼

## *Ernest Hemingway to His Father*
## 欧内斯特·海明威致父亲

Hendaye, France, 14 September 1927

Dear Dad,

Thanks very much for your letter and for forwarding the letter to Uncle Tyley. I had a good letter from him yesterday. You cannot know how badly I feel about having caused you and Mother so much shame and suffering—but I could not write you about all of my and Hadley's troubles even if it were the thing to do. It takes two weeks for a letter to cross the Atlantic and I have tried not to transfer all the hell I have been through to anyone by letter. I love Hadley and I love Bumby—Hadley and I split up—I did not desert her nor was I committing adultery with anyone. I was living in the apartment with Bumby—looking after him while Hadley was away on a trip and it was when she came back from this trip that she decided she wanted the definite divorce. We arranged everything and there was no scandal and no disgrace. Our trouble had been going on for a long time. It was entirely my fault and it is no one's business. I have nothing but love admiration and respect for Hadley and while we are busted up I have not in any way lost Bumby. He lived with me

　　亲爱的父亲：

　　非常感谢您的来信以及帮忙转交信件给泰勒叔叔。我昨天收到了一封他寄来的充满善意的信。您无法知道，我对自己给您和母亲带来如此多的羞辱和痛苦是感到多么的糟糕——但我没法写信告诉您关于我和哈德利之间所有的问题，即使那是我应该做的。一封信跨越大西洋需要花费两个星期的时间，而且我尽量不要把我所经历过的痛苦通过书信转移给任何人。我爱哈德利和邦比——哈德利和我离婚了——我并没有遗弃她，也没有与任何人通奸。我之前一直和邦比住在公寓里——哈德利外出旅行时，我一直照顾着他。而当她旅行回来时，她决定想要跟我明确地提出离婚。我们安排好了一切，没有流言蜚语，也没有耻辱。我们之间的问题由来已久，冰冻三尺非一日之寒。这全部是我的过错，与他人无关。对于哈德利，我除了敬仰和尊重，别无其他。当我们的婚姻破裂时，我无论如何不能失去邦比。离婚后，邦比和我一起居住在瑞士，他11月份将会回来陪我在山里过冬。

in Switzerland after the divorce and he is coming back in November and will spend this winter with me in the mountains.

You are fortunate enough to have only been in love with one woman in your life. For over a year I had been in love with two people and had been absolutely faithful to Hadley. When Hadley decided that we had better get a divorce the girl with whom I was in love was in America. I had not heard from her for almost two months. In her last letter she had said that we must not think of each other but of Hadley. You refer to "Love Pirates," "persons who break up your home etc." and you know that I am hot tempered but I know that it is easy to wish people in Hell when you know nothing of them. I have seen, suffered, and been through enough so that I do not wish anyone in Hell. It is because I do not want you to suffer with ideas of shame and disgrace that I now write all this. We have not seen much of each other for a long time and in the meantime our lives have been going on and there has been a year of tragedy in mine and I know you can appreciate how difficult and almost impossible it is for me to write about it.

After we were divorced, if Hadley would have wanted me, I would have gone back to her. She said that things were better as they were and that we were both better off. I will never stop loving Hadley nor Bumby nor will I cease to look after them. I will never stop loving Pauline Pfeiffer to whom I am married. I have now responsibility toward three people instead of one. Please understand this and know that it doesn't make it easier to write about it. I do understand how hard it is for you to have to make explanations and answer questions and not hear from me. I am a rotten correspondent and it is almost impossible for me to write about my private affairs. Without seeking

您非常幸运，一生中只爱一个女人。在一年多的时间里，我同时爱上两个人，但我绝对忠实于哈德利。当哈德利决定我们最好离婚时，我爱的那个女孩正在美国。我已经差不多有两个月时间没有收到她的来信了。在她的上一封信里，她说道，我们不能只考虑彼此，而应该考虑考虑哈德利。您提到"爱情女强盗"、"破坏您的家庭的人"等等，您知道我脾气急躁，但是我知道，当一个人不了解别人时，很容易诅咒他们进地狱。可我已经目睹了、遭受了并经历了足够的痛苦，因此我不会诅咒任何人进地狱。正是因为我不希望您承受羞愧和耻辱等思想的包袱，现在我才给您写信说明这一切。我们已有很长一段时间没有见面了，与此同时，我们的生活还在继续，发生在我身上的悲剧已有一年了。我知道您能理解，对我来说，将这一切写出来有多么困难，几乎不可能。

我们离婚后，假如哈德利还需要我，我将会回到她的身边。但她说情况有所好转，已如过去一样，我们俩也都渐入佳境。我将永远不会停止对哈德利和邦比的爱，也不会停止对他们的照顾。我也永远不会停止对与我结婚的宝琳·费孚的爱。现在，我对三个人而不只是对一个人负有责任。请您理解这一切，并理解我写出这一切并不会更轻松。我真的理解，您不得不向别人解释和回答别人的提问，加上又收不到我的信，这一切对您来说有多么困难。我是一个糟糕的通信者，对我来说，把我的私事写出来几乎是不可能的。没有刻意追求——凭借我的作品的成功——由此带来的所有收益，我已转交给哈德利——包括美国、英国、德国、斯堪的纳维亚半岛上的国家——因为这一切，又引起了一堆的闲言碎语。我根本不在乎这些闲话，您也不必在乎。我已经回归自我，人们所谈论的关于我的每一个空想和诽谤类的故事，都是没有根据的。这

it—through the success of my books—all the profits of which I have turned over to Hadley—both in America, England, Germany and the Scandinavian countries—because of all this there is a great deal of talk. I pay no attention to any of it and neither must you. I have had come back to me, stories people have told about me of every fantastic and scandalous sort—all without foundation. These sorts of stories spring up about all writers—ball players—popular evangelists or any public performers. But it is through the desire to keep my own private life to myself—to give no explanations to anybody—and not to be a public performer personally that I have unwittingly caused you great anxiety. The only way I could keep my private life to myself was to keep it to myself—and I did owe you and Mother a statement on it. But I can't write about it all the time.

I know you don't like the sort of thing I write but that is the difference in our taste and all the critics are not Fanny Butcher. I know that I am not disgracing you in my writing but rather doing something that some day you will be proud of. I can't do it all at once. I feel that eventually my life will not be a disgrace to you either. It also takes a long time to unfold.

You would be so much happier and I would too if you could have confidence in me. When people ask about me, say that Ernie never tells us anything about his private life or even where he is but only writes that he is working hard. Don't feel responsible for what I write or what I do. I take the responsibility, I make the mistakes and I take the punishment.

类故事涌现在每一个作家、运动员、受欢迎的福音传道士或任何公众表演者的身上。但由于我渴望拥有属于自己的私人生活——我没有对任何人做出解释——而且就个人而言,我不愿成为一个公众表演者。我的行为却在不知不觉中给您带来了巨大的焦虑。唯一使我拥有属于自己的私人生活的办法,就是把它保留给自己——对于这件事,我的确欠您和母亲一个解释,但我不能总是写信谈论它。

我知道您不喜欢我写的那种类型的作品,但那是我们的品味有所不同,而且并非所有的评论家都是范妮·布彻。我知道我没有在我的作品中让您蒙羞,而是做了一件将来某一天会令您引以为傲的事。我不能立刻做到。我觉得我的生活最终也将不会给您带来耻辱。这同样需要很长一段时间才能展示出来。

如果您对我充满信心,您会感到快乐得多,我也会感到快乐得多。当人们问起我,您就说欧尼从来不告诉我们他的私人生活,甚至不告诉我们他在哪里,而只是写信说他在努力工作。您不必觉得要为我所写的或者我所做的事情负责。我自己承担责任,我犯了错误,我接受惩罚,一人做事一人当。

1927 年 9 月 14 日
写于法国,昂达伊

## William Cullen Bryant to His Mother
## 威廉·库伦·布莱恩特致母亲

(June, 1821)

Dear Mother,

I hasten to send you the melancholy intelligence of what has lately happened to me.

Early on the evening of the eleventh day of the present month, I was at a neighboring house in this village. Several people of both sexes were assembled in one of the apartments, and three or four others, with myself, were in another. At last came in a little elderly gentleman, pale, thin, with a solemn countenance, hooked nose, and hollow eyes. It was not long before we were summoned to attend in the apartment where he and the rest of the company were gathered. We went in and took our seats; the little elderly gentleman with the hooked nose prayed, and we all stood up. When he had finished, most of us sat down. The gentleman with the hooked nose then muttered certain cabalistical expressions which I was too much frightened to remember, but I recollect that at the conclusion I was given to understand that I was married to a young lady of the name of Frances Fairchild, whom I perceived standing

　　亲爱的母亲：

　　我匆忙给您寄去这封信，是想告诉您最近发生在我身上的一件令人
郁闷的事情。

　　这个月 11 号那天的傍晚时分，我刚好在与村子相邻的一栋房子里。
有几个男女聚集在其中一间屋里，而我自己跟其他三四个人则待在另外
一间里。最后，进来了一位年纪稍长的小个子先生，他脸色苍白、身材
瘦削，有着一副严肃的面孔、如鹰钩般的鼻子以及一双空洞的眼睛。不
一会儿，我们被人召唤到另外那间屋子里去，那位先生和其他人都聚集
在那里。我们走进去，坐了下来。那位鹰钩鼻小个子先生开始作祷告，
我们全体起立。他作完祷告之后，我们多数人都坐了下来。接着，那位
鹰钩鼻先生口中念念有词，讲了些神秘的话语。我当时非常害怕，以至
于没有记住他到底说了些什么。但是我记得在结束的时候，我被告知自
己已经和一个名叫弗朗西丝·菲切尔德的姑娘结婚了。我感觉得到她当
时就站在我身边，我希望几个月后能荣幸地把她作为您的儿媳妇介绍给
您。这是一件令那个可怜的姑娘感兴趣的事，她的父母均已不在人世……

by my side, and I hope in the course of a few months to have the pleasure of introducing to you as your daughter-in-law, which is a matter of some interest to the poor girl, who has neither father nor mother in the world...

I looked only for goodness of heart, an ingenuous and affectionate disposition, a good understanding, etc., and the character of my wife is too frank and single-hearted to suffer me to fear that I may be disappointed. I do myself wrong; I did not look for these nor any other qualities, but they trapped me before I was aware, and now I am married in spite of myself.

Thus the current of destiny carries us along. None but a madman would swim against the stream, and none but a fool would exert himself to swim with it. The best way is to float quietly with the tide...

Your affectionate son,

William

　　我所要寻找的对象，只要求她心地善良、性情直率、重感情、温柔体贴等。而我的妻子为人过于坦率和单纯，我害怕自己会失望。我自己做错了，我并没有去寻求这些或那些品质，但是在我自己还未意识到之前，却已掉入了他们的圈套，身不由己地结婚了。

　　命运的潮流正是这样带领着我们一直向前的。除了疯子，没人会逆流而上；除了傻子，也没人会竭力与潮共舞。最好的办法就是静静地随波逐流……

您深情的儿子：威廉

写于 1821 年 6 月

Barcelona

Wednesday, 2:00 P. M.

22 October, 1908

My dear parents,

The worst is behind us! That was last night's organ concert and the lecture preceding it. Quite frankly I was somewhat worried about this lecture since I am not used to giving long talks in French?? and the hall is enormous: three thousand people. But to my amazement I discovered that I felt as much at home in French as I do in German and that it was easier for me to speak loudly and clearly in French than in German! I stood there without a manuscript, and within three minutes I sensed that I had captured my audience more surely than I had ever done before. I spoke for fifty-five minutes, and next came an organ recital that lasted for one hour. I have never been so successful. When the program ended, they all remained in their seats. I had to go back to my organ and play for another half hour. The audience was sorry to leave... it was half-past midnight!

Here, the concerts are announced for 9:15, but at that time there's not a

名人小课堂

阿尔贝特·施韦泽（Albert Schweitzer, 1875 ~ 1965 年）

德国哲学家、神学家、医生、管风琴演奏家、社会活动家、人道主义者。1904 年，在哲学、神学和音乐方面已经拥有巨大声望的他听到刚果缺少医生的呼吁，决定到非洲行医。1913 年他来到非洲，在加蓬的兰巴雷内建立了丛林诊所，服务非洲直至逝世。1952 年，他获得了诺贝尔和平奖，被称为"非洲之子"。

亲爱的父母亲：

最坏的时刻已经过去了！我指的是昨晚的管风琴音乐会以及音乐会前的演讲。坦白讲，我多少有点担心这次演讲，因为我不习惯用法语作长篇演讲，加之音乐厅非常大，坐了有 3000 人。但令我感到惊讶的是，我发现自己的法语竟然可以和德语讲得一样熟练，而且对我来说，洪亮清晰地讲法语比讲德语更容易！我站在那儿，没有演讲稿，3 分钟内我比以前任何一次都更确定地感觉到我已经把听众深深地吸引住了。我持续讲了 55 分钟，接下来是持续一个小时的管风琴独奏音乐会。我从未如此成功过。当节目演奏完毕时，所有的听众仍然停留在他们座位上不愿离去，我不得不再次回到管风琴旁，又加演了半小时。当听众们依依不

soul in the auditorium; toward 9:30 the first few people arrive, strolling about in the hall and the lobby, and toward ten o'clock, after three rings of a bell, the people deign to finally take their seats!

On Saturday, a grand concert with organ and orchestra is scheduled in the morning, and I have long rehearsals in the evening, for the organ is very difficult to play since the sound is always delayed. Luckily, I am well rested, and I am managing to overcome the difficulties. Absolutely everyone addresses me as "cheer ma re"; the art critics settle down in the auditorium during rehearsals; my portrait is displayed in the music stores. It's such fun.

I am staying with Walter at the premier hotel on the grand square with splendid palm trees. I have a view of the square and the entire city all the way to the big mountains forty minutes away from here; they are as high as the Hohnack. I walk over to them every afternoon; it takes me a total of two hours.

The weather is the same as at home on a lovely June day. The men who were waiting for me at the railroad station roared with laughter when they saw Walter and me in overcoats.

As I am writing to you, the square below my window is filled with a terrible din. The king is arriving in an hour, and the troops are now taking up their positions. Tomorrow evening there will be a grand gala performance at the theater. I have been invited, but I am not going; I want to rest, for I feel too well to risk my excellent condition.

I will close now; otherwise the letter won't go off tonight. It has to be at the post office by four o'clock. There is no night train to France.

舍地离去时，已是午夜 12 点半了！

　　这里，音乐会虽然通知 9 点 15 分开始，但到了开始的时间，大厅里却不见一个人影；接近 9 点半时，第一批才到了几个人，他们在礼堂或前厅里闲逛，快到 10 点钟时，3 次铃响之后，人们才最终屈尊就座！

　　这个星期六的上午安排了一场由管风琴及管弦乐队演奏的盛大音乐会，前天晚上我花了很长时间彩排，由于管风琴发出的声音总是滞后，所以很难演奏。幸运的是，我休息得很好，精力充沛，成功地设法克服了这些困难。每一个人都称我为"尊敬的艺术大师"；艺术评论家们在彩排期间都认认真真地坐在听众席上；我的画像还被悬挂在许多乐器店里。这多么有趣啊！

　　我与沃尔特住在大广场上的首相宾馆，这里四周环绕着美丽壮观的棕榈树。在房间里，透过窗户我能欣赏到整个广场、整个城市，甚至能一直看到离这儿有 40 分钟路程之遥的群山；那些山与霍荷纳克山一样高。我每天下午步行至山脚下，来回得花费我整整两个小时的时间。

　　此时这里的气候犹如家乡那宜人的 6 月。在火车站，接我的那些人看到我和沃尔特竟还穿着大衣，他们都哈哈大笑起来。

　　就在我给你们写信之际，窗外的广场上人声鼎沸，国王将于一小时后驾到，此刻仪仗队正在列队准备迎接。明天晚上剧院里将举行一场盛大的欢庆表演。我已接到邀请，但我不打算去。我想休息一下，因为我现在感觉很好，我不想冒险破坏我的最佳状态。

　　我得就此搁笔了，否则这封信今晚就寄不出去了。这封信得在 4 点钟之前交到邮局，因为这儿没有开往巴黎的夜班火车。

Please forward this letter to the Ehretsmanns and to the Woytts.

Hugs and kisses,

Albert

请把这封信转交给埃雷茨曼夫妇和沃伊特夫妇。

拥抱、亲吻你们！

阿尔贝特

1908 年 10 月 22 日

星期三，下午 2:00

写于巴塞罗那

*Albert Schweitzer to His Parents* (Ⅱ)

阿尔贝特·施韦泽致父母（2）

Barcelona

Friday, 23 October, 1908

My dear parents,

I have just been asked to participate in the gala concert that will be given on Monday evening in honor of the king and queen. I have accepted. I am to play a Handel concerto for organ and orchestra and the organ part in Bach's Magnificence. The tickets are horrendously expensive. Some of the boxes cost one thousand francs! The net receipts are earmarked for the Catalonian orphans. I am the only soloist in this concert.

I get no chance to write because so much time is wasted here; yesterday's rehearsal dragged on until 12:30 A.M.! Today from 2:00 to 6:00! No one ever hurries, and they all smoke constantly. No sooner have we rehearsed for ten minutes than the conductor sits down, rolls himself a cigarette, and smokes it, and the instrumentalists do likewise... and they don't continue rehearsing until the cigarette has been smoked. Paul could see fiddlers galore here, each

亲爱的父母亲：

我刚刚被邀请参加下周一晚上为国王和王后举行的庆祝音乐会。我接受了这一邀请。我将为管风琴和管弦乐演奏一段韩德尔的协奏曲，管风琴部分则演奏巴赫的《辉煌》。这场音乐会的票价贵得要命，有些包厢卖到 1000 法郎！音乐会的纯收入将指定为加泰罗尼亚的孤儿的专款专用。我是本场音乐会唯一的独奏者。

我没有机会写信，因为许多时间都白白地浪费在这儿了。昨天的彩排一直拖到上午 12 点半！今天则从 2 点拖到 6 点！没有一个人抓紧时间的，而且他们还时不时地抽烟。我们彩排还不到 10 分钟，乐队指挥就坐下来，为自己卷了支烟，抽了起来，于是乐手们也有样学样……直到香烟抽完了，他们才继续彩排。保罗可以看到小提琴手们聚集在这里，每个人嘴角都叼着一支香烟在那浪费时间。一开始我对如此浪费时间的行

fiddling away with a cigarette in the corner of his mouth. At first I was annoyed at the waste of time, but now I am quite domesticated, and I smile.

The newspapers have reported very positively on my lecture and my recital. On Saturday evening the auditorium will be sold out. I live very sensibly. I have just taken a big two-hour stroll along the large ring street, which runs from the hotel to the mountains. No rehearsal tomorrow morning! I'll sleep, write... and take a walk.

Yesterday I was amazed to see that they don't take anything like the same security measure for the monarchs as in Germany. The crowd thronged around the king's carriage, so it could advance only at a walking pace. Freedom reigns here. They did not even clear the streets for the military parade. A woman with a donkey cart held up an entire regiment.It was too comical. We went to the harbor—immensely huge—to see the French squadron.

The city and the people generally make the best impression. Everything is clean, everyone works.

It is ten-thirty at night. I am writing to you by the open window... the large palm trees are swaying in the wind.

I embrace you with all my heart,

Albert

为感到气愤，但我现在相当习以为常了，一笑置之。

报界对我的演讲及独奏会进行了高度肯定的报道。星期六晚上，音乐会的门票将出售一空。我过得非常潇洒。我刚刚沿着从宾馆至群山的环形大街散了两个小时的步。明天早上没有彩排！我可以睡睡觉、写写信……还有散散步。

昨天，我看到他们竟然没有采取任何像在德国为君主采取的那些安保措施，我感到非常惊奇。人群蜂拥在国王的马车周围，马车只能以步行的速度缓缓前行。这里充满了自由。他们甚至没有为军队的检阅肃清街道。一个赶着驴车的妇女挡住了整个阅兵团。真是太滑稽了。我们还去了港口——非常大的港口——去看法国的海军舰队。

这个城市和这儿的人们普遍地给我留下了最好的印象。这里每件事物都是干净的，每个人都在工作。

现在是晚上 10 点半。我正在敞开的窗下给你们写信……高大的棕榈树在风中摇曳。

我全身心地拥抱你们。

阿尔贝特
1908 年 10 月 23 日，星期五
写于巴塞罗那

## Chapter 3

# 有一种温暖从未离开

*Never stop smiling, not even when you are sad, someone might fall in love with your smile. A smile is the most charming part of a person forever.*

永远都不要停止微笑，即使是在你难过的时候，说不定有人会爱上你的笑容。微笑永远是一个人身上最好看的东西。

## *Ogden Nash to His Daughter*
## 奥格登·纳什致女儿

February 6, 1939

My sweet girls,

I wish so that you were here with us. The next time we must surely bring you along, so remember to practice your manners and learn to eat all sorts of food. Paris is full of children. There are lots of parks, and every park is full of boys and girls on bicycles and roller skates, or playing football and other games all day long. Also, I think everybody in Paris has a dog, but none of them are as pretty as Spangle. A beautiful river, the Seine, runs right through the middle of the city, and Mummy and I have already counted 22 bridges that cross it. Don't you think that you could have fun here? The French children are very polite, as everyone is in France, and I am sure you would enjoy playing with them; so, Linell, you must pay great attention to your French teacher and learn very fast, in order to be able to understand well when you come here. You might teach Isable some of what you learn, too.

There are many, many interesting things to see here. Paris is a very old city, and today Mummy and I saw a beautiful building, that was started by the

名人小课堂

奥格登·纳什（Ogden Nash, 1902 ~ 1971）

美国诗人。纳什的诗风非常独特，对 20 世纪的美国洞察深刻，评论精辟，被称为"稀有诗人"、"最滑稽的诗人"、"幽默语言大师"、"上帝赐与美国的礼物"等。代表作品有《自由旋转》、《享乐之路》及《1929 年以来的诗歌》等。他的作品在全世界都具有很大的影响力。

我可爱的女孩们：

我非常希望你们能与我们一起来这里。下次我们一定会把你们一起带上，所以你们要记住要多多练习礼仪并学会吃各种类型的食物。巴黎这里到处都是小孩，还有许多的公园，而且公园里整天都有许多小孩，男孩女孩都有，他们在这里骑自行车、滑旱冰，或者踢足球和玩其他游戏。还有，我认为巴黎的每个人都有一条狗，但没有一条狗能像斯潘格那样漂亮。这有一条美丽的河流，塞纳河，它正好从市中心穿过。妈咪和我已经数过了，河上有 22 座桥。难道你们不认为你们可以在这里玩得很开心吗？如每一个法国人一样，法国的孩子非常有礼貌，我保证你们会非常喜欢与他们一起玩耍；所以，利内尔，你必须注意听你法语教师的课，这样就可以学得很快，以便你来这里后能很好地理解法文。你也可以教伊莎贝尔一些你所学到的东西。

这里有许许多多有趣的东西可以看。巴黎是一个非常古老的城市，今天妈咪和我去看了一栋非常美丽的建筑。它是 1600 多年前由罗马人开

Romans more than 1600 years ago. It is called Cluny. We have also been to the Louvre, a museum now full of the most beautiful paintings and statues. But years ago, the kings and queens of France used to live there, until the French people got angry with them and chopped off their heads.

This afternoon we went to a beautiful cathedral on an island in the middle of the river. It is called the Cathedral of the Dame, which means the cathedral of Our Lady the Virgin. It is more than 900 years old, and so high that you can hardly see the top. The windows are of gorgeous stained glass, red and blue and yellow and green and purple, so that they cast light like a rainbow on the walls. A very good king of France who lived 700 years ago and later became Saint Louis was buried (from) there. Tell Delia that we offered a candle to the Virgin Mary for each of you there, and that we are bringing her back a rosary from there also. Mummy and I climbed the tower later. We were very tired when we got to the top, but it was interesting. Some hideous stone gargoyles were looking right into our faces, so we looked down at Paris lying at our feet, and it was beautiful. We could see miles of river, and the bridges and the lovely old buildings. It is warmer here than at home, but sometimes the fogs so thick that even the taxi drivers get lost; last night three of them ran right off the street and into the fountains on the Rond Point on the Champs Elysees, which Boppy can tell you about. It must have been very damp and uncomfortable for the passengers.

I think you would like the French trains. We rode on one from Le Havre to Paris, just like the one that Gaston et Josephine took when they were leaving for America. When the engine whistles it says tweet instead of toot, and the porters are very polite.

始建造的，它的名字叫做克卢尼。我们也去了卢浮宫这个装满最美丽的绘画和雕塑的博物馆。但是许多年以前，法国历代的国王和王后曾住在那里，直到法国人民愤怒起义，砍掉了他们的头。

今天下午，我们去了位于河中央的岛上的一座美丽的教堂，它的名字叫做巴黎圣母院，意思是我们圣母玛利亚的教堂。它已有 900 多年的历史。教堂很高，几乎看不到顶。窗户是用绚丽的彩色玻璃做的，有红色、蓝色、黄色、绿色和紫色，所以玻璃把光投射到墙上就像彩虹一样。700 年前，有一位非常好的法国国王，后来成为圣路易斯，他就埋在那儿。告诉迪莉娅，在那里，我们替你们每个人向圣母玛利亚献了一支蜡烛，并且我们从那里带回了一串念珠给她。后来，妈咪和我爬上了塔楼。当我们爬到塔顶时，我们累坏了，但这很有趣。一些可怕的石像魔鬼正眼对着我们，所以我们转而俯视脚下的巴黎，它十分美丽。我们能看到数英里长的河流、河上的桥以及可爱的古老建筑。这里的气候比家乡要暖和一些，但有时浓雾弥漫，就连出租车司机都会迷路。昨晚，三辆出租车开出街道，驶入了位于切普斯·艾利瑟斯街的街心喷泉池中，博普会告诉你们这件事。车上的乘客们身上一定湿透了，非常不舒服。

我想你们会喜欢法国的火车的。我们坐上了一列从勒阿弗尔到巴黎的火车，这列火车与加斯顿和约瑟芬他们去美国时乘坐的火车很像。引擎发动的时候，汽笛发出"吱吱"的声音而不是"嘟嘟"声，而且乘务员非常有礼貌。

你们也会喜欢船的。船上有一个小剧院，每天下午那里会上演木偶剧给孩子们看，而且甲板上有足够的空间给孩子们跑来跑去玩耍。有时候，风刮得很猛，海浪汹涌，船就会有些摇晃，但那很有趣，就像荡秋千一样。在我们的旅行中，有一个年仅 14 岁的小姑娘，她因为小提琴拉得很出色而出名，她的名字叫吉拉·布斯塔波。有一天晚上，在节日音

Yon would like the boat, too. There is a little theatre where there are puppet shows for children every afternoon, and there is plenty of room to run and play on the decks. Sometimes, when the wind blows hard and the sea is rough, the boat joggles a little bit, but that is good fun, like being in as swing. On our trip there was a little girl only 14 years old who is already famous because she plays the violin so beautifully. Her name is Guila Bustabo, and she played for us one night, at the gala concert, where everybody gave money to help the old sailors. French sailors have very pink cheeks indeed, and speak very fast, and I don't think they ever get old. Really, so I am not sure who got the money.

I must tell you that whenever you walk along the banks of the Seine, you see dozens of old men fishing with long, long poles. I don't think they ever catch anything, but they have a lovely time thinking about what they might catch just supposing there were any fish there. We'll try it when you come here with us. Perhaps we'll catch the first fish ever to be caught there.

I adore you both, my darlings,

And don't forget me.

Daddy

乐会上，她为我们演奏，每个人都出了钱用以帮助那些老水手。事实上，法国水手们脸颊红润，说话很快，我不觉得他们会变老。真的，所以我无法肯定谁得到了那些钱。

我必须告诉你们，无论什么时候，沿着塞纳河岸走，你都能看见许多的老人拿着很长很长的鱼杆在那钓鱼。我想他们什么也没有钓到，但是他们只要心中坚定信念，想着那儿有鱼，可能会钓到鱼，他们就过得很开心了。等你们到这儿和我们一起时，我们也去试一试。也许我们会在所有人当中，钓到这里的第一条鱼呢。

我爱你们俩，亲爱的，

不要忘记我。

爸爸

写于 1939 年 2 月 6 日

# Winston Churchill to His Daughter
## (Mary Churchill)
# 温斯顿·丘吉尔致女儿
## （玛丽·丘吉尔）

My darling Mary,

"Many Happy Returns of the Day." This should reach you on your Birthday the 15th. but if it comes earlier or later it carries with it the fondest love of your Father. I have watched with admiration and respect the career of distinction and duty what you have made for yourself during the hard years of the war. I look forward in the days that may be left me to see you happy and glorious in peace. You are a great joy to your mother and me and we are hoping that very soon you will be living with us at Chart well and in our new house in London. It will be lovely having you with us.

Here it is sunshine and calm. I paint all day and every day and have banished care and disillusionment to the shades. Alex came and painted too. He is very good. Monsieur Montag is coming to comment and guide me in a few days. I have three nice pictures so far, and am now off to seek for another. Sarah is writing you herself.

With all my affection

Your loving Father

Winston S. Churchill

亲爱的玛丽：

"祝你生日快乐，年年有今日，岁岁有今朝！"这封信应该可以在15号你生日那天到达你手中，但不管它早到或迟到，都带着你父亲最深情的爱。我一直带着赞赏与尊重的目光看待你在艰苦的战争岁月中为自己所创立的非凡的业绩和承担的职责。在我有生之年，我期待看到你在和平的日子过得幸福辉煌。你是你母亲与我的巨大快乐，我们盼望着很快你就能和我们在查特维尔庄园和伦敦的新居共同生活。有你同我们在一起一定会很好。

这里阳光灿烂，一片宁静。我整天作画，每天如此，这让我消除了烦恼，也对阴暗的事物也浮想联翩。亚历克斯也到这里来画画，他人很好。蒙塔格先生过几天会来给我点评与指导。到目前为止，我已完成了三幅好画。现在我开始为另一幅作品寻找题材。此时，萨拉正在亲自给你写信。

给你我全部的情感

爱你的父亲

温斯顿·S·丘吉尔

# Ernest Hemingway to His Daughter
## (Mary Hemingway)
# 欧内斯特·海明威致女儿
## （玛丽·海明威）

Torcello, 20 November 1948

Dearest Kittner,

Been working hard and missing you harder. No mails today at all. I wrote you day before yesterday and forwarded a letter from your family to the Excelsior in Firenze today. Now writing you just at sun-set. Been beautiful fall weather ever since the day you left. I went shooting with Emilio and shot 25 small birds and we might have gotten two ducks as four flashed over us very low but were eating lunch when it happened. Might have missed them too.

Have my correspondence all done except for letter to Rice. Then will do the article. May do the article and then Rice since will have to go into Venice to get Power of Attorney notarized. Wrote Charley Ritz too.

There is a big duck shoot either tomorrow (Sunday) a.m. or else Monday. Emilio is going to let me know tonight. Hope it's Monday as my shoulder is sore from those high, straight up and down shots. I think those are probably quite heavy loads of the light shot. Can really shoot that over and under now.

最亲爱的基特纳：

我一直努力地工作着，而且更想你了。今天，我连一封邮件也没有收到。我前天给你写了封信，今天又从你的家转寄了一封到罗佛伦萨艾塞斯尔的信。现在是日落时分，我正在给你写信。自你离开的那天起，这里一直是秋高气爽、气候宜人。我和埃米利奥去打猎了，共捕获了 25 只小鸟。有四只野鸭从我们头上低低地飞过，但是当时我们正在吃午饭，要不我们有可能打到两只野鸭，也有可能一只也打不到。

除了写给赖斯的信之外，我已处理完我所有的信件。接着我要开始写那篇文章。也许我会先写文章，再给赖斯写信，因为我一会得去威尼斯办理授权书证明。我也给查理·里兹写了一封信。

明天（星期天）上午或者星期一，我们将有一场野鸭大猎杀。埃米利奥今晚会让我知道确切的时间。我希望星期一去，由于我的肩膀因向高处射击，重复地直直抬起和放下猎枪而感到酸痛。我想那可能是负荷

Haven't started learning the double yet.

Believe magazines etc. held up by the dock strike. They say over 50 000 sacks of mail on the docks in NY. But you read the papers too so won't Kalten born the news to you.

Your last pictures (the tower etc.) came out excellently. Got them last night.

No more word from Childies.

Hope your news was good.

I've been trying to stay awake and read until midnight or one a.m.

No local news. Mooky's foot got ok. Ate outdoors in the sun today and he kept his head in my lap all through lunch; clams, sole, white rice plain. Bobby the other dog, Crazy's brother, can sit up to beg and also make a how do you do and a Fancy Meeting You.

There's nobody living here now. Today three couples for lunch though??a character who was either a fairy or a cinema star or both with reconditioned woman (fenders straightened, bad paint job), a sort of Brusadelli type with woman to match and a brace of Belgiums. I can now tell the travelling Belgium as far as can smell them.

Best to all your friends. Love to my kitten. Be good and have good fun. It's dark now and the shooting has started. Been trying to think what a Belgium smells like (the post-war travelling Belgiums) think it is a blend of traitorous King, toe jam, un-washed navels, old bicycle saddles, (sweated) paving stones,

太重。我现在已经能真正地掌握立式猎枪射击的技巧了。我还没有开始学双管枪射击。

相信杂志之类的东西已经因为码头工人罢工而受阻。他们说有5万多麻布袋的邮件滞留在纽约码头。但你也看过这些报道，所以我不用再把这些消息详细转告给你。

你最新的摄影作品（塔之类）照得非常好。我昨晚收到它们的。

没有奇尔狄斯的消息。

希望你的消息都是好的。

我一直在努力保持清醒，看书看到午夜或凌晨1点。

没有当地的消息。穆基的脚已经好了。我今天在户外的阳光下吃午饭，那只米白色的小狗一直把头放在我的膝盖上。它静静地独自待着。另一只小狗博比，即克雷兹的兄弟，能坐起来讨好，也会做"你好"和"见到你真高兴"等动作。

现在已经没有别的人住在这儿了。不过今天有三对夫妇在这儿吃午饭：一个像童话里的人物，或像电影明星，或许两者都是，他带着一个打扮过的女人（后背挺得直直的，浓妆艳抹），一个像布鲁斯代尔类型的男人带着一个女人，还有一对比利时夫妇。只要闻一下，我就知道他们从比利时来旅游的。

向你所有的朋友问好。我爱你，我的小猫咪。祝你身体健康、生活愉快。现在，天已经黑了，外面的枪声已经响起。我一直在努力回想比利时人闻起来像什么（战后的比利时旅行者），我想它是一种混合味，融合了叛变的国王、拥挤的脚趾、没有洗的肚脐、破旧自行车的座板、（浸

and eminently sound money with a touch of leek soup and cooking parsnips.

I love you dearest Kittner and miss you very, very very very, very, very much.

Papa

着汗）铺路的石子、大量钱财，以及一点儿韭葱汤和烹调用的欧洲防风草的味道。

我爱你，最亲爱的基特纳，我非常非常，非常非常，非常非常想念你。

爸爸
写于托切罗
1948 年 11 月 20 日

*Eugene O'Neill to His Son*

# 尤金·奥尼尔致儿子

June 20th 1936

Dear Eugene,

It was good to get your letter. I would have written you, only you said in your wire you were writing, so I waited to learn all the details of your good news. And it sure is good news! But, as I wired you, I was by no means astonished, or anything like that, that you had done so nobly, for your somber premonitions had not impressed me as being liable to coincide with the facts when they appeared. I know such dreary forebodings too damned well. They are the familiar spirits of this branch of the O'Neills—one of the baneful heritages you get from me, I'm afraid. I've been enjoying more than my usual share of them lately, too, what with this Cycle of plays stretching out into a future of seemingly endless hard labor. It looks now as if there would have to be still another play—a ninth which will carry me back to 1770 as a starter.

What you write about the exams is damned interesting and I am glad you told me so much about the oral. Of course, I knew there was one, but had no idea it was such a formidable inquisition. I can imagine how you felt when you

**名人·小课堂**

尤金·奥尼尔（Eugene O'Neill, 1888 ~ 1953 年）

美国著名剧作家。他是一位多产作家，一生创作独幕剧 21 部，多幕剧 28 部。其中优秀剧作有：《东航卡迪夫》《加勒比斯之月》《天边外》《安娜·克利斯蒂》《琼斯皇帝》等。1936 年凭借代表作《天边外》获诺贝尔文学奖。

亲爱的尤金：

很高兴收到你的来信。我本该已经给你写完信的，只是你在电话里说你正写信给我，所以我就等着了解你的好消息的所有细节。这确实是好消息！但是，当我从电话中得知你干得如此出色时，我并不感到惊讶或者任何类似那样的感觉。我并未在意你的不祥预感，因为当事实发生的时候，它们是很容易与之相一致的。我对那些可恶的不祥预感了如指掌。那是我们这支奥尼尔家族成员常见的情绪——恐怕这是你从我这里继承的有害遗传因子之一。我近期也一直遇到这种情况，而且比以前还要糟。因为，这部系列剧越往后面发展，这烦人的工作似乎越没完没了。现在看起来好像还得接下去写另一部剧本——第九部剧本，这部剧本一开始将要把我带回至 1770 年。

你在信里所讲的关于考试的事情相当有趣，我很高兴你如此详尽地告诉我关于口试的情况。当然，我知道有口试这回事，但并没想到它竟是一种如此可怕的询问。我可以想象得到当时你在大厅中走来走去，等

paced the hall waiting for the verdict!

As for the job, from what you tell me, that assuredly is a grand bit of good fortune! And the salary is more than I ever thought you would get to start with.

Speaking of money, you know, I hope that if ever you get in a tough spot I can always manage to come across with something, although, as you may guess, the next couple of years will be lean ones unless that rarity for me, a movie rights purchase, comes up. I want to tell you frankly what my exact situation is. Whatever income I have from investments is more than abolished by the alimony dole. That means that as far as my half of Carlotta's and my household expenses, etc. is concerned I am living on capital and will be for the next two years or more, for I do not expect to be able to release any new play for production or publication before then. Royalties on books bring in something but comparatively little. Stock, amateur performances' royalties don't amount to much because my plays are difficult to cast and seldom attempted. Foreign productions continue to be flatteringly constant— but are done in repertoire for a few performances at a time, and with half to a translator, tax, etc. the return to me in dollars is negligible, or less. I had hoped something from the London production of Ah, Wilderness! by the Irish Group Theatre, but in spite of a unanimously enthusiastic critical reception, no one is going to see it and it has possibly closed by this.

So that's about the situation—and it is due to grow steadily worse instead of better, pending the appearance of my new work. I tell you all this not to cry poor, you understand, but to present the hard facts.

I am determined, if I go broke in the process, not to release any play of the Cycle until I have at least three or four in final form, and more in first

待结论时是怎样的感觉。

说到工作，从你告诉我的内容来看，那无疑是一个很好的运气！而且薪水比我曾经设想过的你一开始能拿到的要高一些。

说到钱，你知道的，我希望假如你真的遇到什么困难时，我总是可以尽力提供帮助——尽管你也可能猜到，今后的两三年里我会比较拮据，除非有人想要购买我的电影版权，不过这种事很罕见。我想坦率地告诉你我的实际情况。无论我的投资能获得多少收益，都不够赡养费这一项开支。那意味着就我所承担的夏洛特一半的赡养费以及家庭的各项开支等而言，我现在是在吃老本，而且今后两年或更长的时间内也将如此，因为，在那之前，我不期望我的任何一个新剧本可以上演或出版。书的版税能带来些许收入，但相当少。股票、业余演出的使用费也非常有限，因为我的剧本上演的难度很大，而且很少有人尝试。在国外，我的剧本倒是经常继续在上演，颇受追捧——但演出的是保留剧目，一次演几场。一半的收入用于支付译者稿酬、交税等，最后以美元返回给我的钱是微不足道的，或者更少。我原本寄希望于爱尔兰群体剧团在伦敦上演的《啊，荒野！》会给我带来收益，但是尽管该剧引起广泛而热烈的评论反应，却没有一个人去看，这样的话，演出可能已经终止了。

这就是我的实际情况——而且在等待我的新作品问世期间，这情形会逐步地恶化，而不是好转。你明白的，我告诉你这一切并不是哭穷，而是向你陈述困难的事实。

假如在这个过程中我破产了，我也决不会将这个剧本系列中的任何一本发布出来，除非这个系列我至少有三四部剧本已经定稿了，其他的剧本已经有了初稿。对我来说，这是必要的，因为，我所重视的当然是

draft. This is essential to me because the emphasis with me is naturally on the work as a whole, not on its separate parts. It is also essential for the stage production of the work as a whole that the Guild have several plays to plan on as a starter—for they intend to get together a special repertoire company just to do this Cycle, and when it comes to tying up actors and actresses for three or four years, in these days of Talkie temptation, you've got to show them parts in several plays that make it to their advantage to sign up. You can't do it on one or two plays with a vague promise of good parts in plays not yet written, no matter who the author. The plan, as I guess I've told you before, is to do two plays a season.

So you see how this Cycle has me involved in a hell of a lot of labor—and costly time—before I can expect any returns of any kind. You will also appreciate that I have many low days of O'Neill heebie-jeebies when I feel very old and tired, and doubt myself and my work, and wonder why in hell something in me drove me on to undertake such a hellish job when I might have coasted along and just written some more plays, as a well-behaved playwright does.

But enough of that.

I foresaw that you would probably get some tart retorts from the Middle West on your article. Midwesterners are very sensitive people—that is, in one respect.

Love to you and Betty from us—and a sweet kiss from Blemie to Cabot.

Father

这项工作作为一个整体，而不是它的各个部分，这对于将整个系列剧在舞台上的演出也一样必要。盖尔德剧团已经计划上演好几部戏作为事业的开始，因为他们为了演出这个系列剧而打算组织一个专门的戏剧团。而且，男女演员的选定也要花上三四年时间。在如今有声电影对演员造成巨大诱惑的情况下，你得拿出几部剧本里的某些片段给他们看看，这样才会有利于他们签协议。要是只依靠一两个剧本，含糊地承诺剧本里还未写好的精彩内容，那么，不论作者是谁，你都不会获得成功。如我猜想我之前告诉过你的，我的计划是每个季度写两个剧本。

因此，你瞧，在我可以期待得到任何回报之前，这个系列剧已经使我陷入了无穷无尽的工作之中，还要花费大量的时间。你也将会理解，我度过了许多奥尼尔家族特有的那种紧张兮兮的日子。我觉得自己老了，也累了，开始怀疑自己以及自己的工作。而且我想知道，究竟为什么我内心中的某种东西会一直驱使我去承担这样一件可怕的工作。我本可以随意地向前生活下去，像一些举止大方的剧作家那样，只是多写一些剧本。

嗯，说得够多了。

我已经预见你的文章很可能会在中西部受到一些尖酸的反驳。中西部的人非常敏感——在某一方面是如此。

献上我们的爱给你和贝蒂，以及来自布莱米的一个甜甜的吻带给卡伯特。

爸爸
1936 年 6 月 20 日

*John O'hara to His Daughter*
*(Wylie O'hara)*

约翰·奥哈拉致女儿
（威利·奥哈拉）

Princeton

7th January1962, Sunday

My dear,

I have been thinking about our conversation of last night, and I hope you have too.

1962, in some ways, is Wylie O'hara's Year of Decision. Some of the decisions you make this year will have an important bearing on decisions you may want to make several years hence.

For example: suppose that when you are 20 or 21, you should discover that you want to participate in one of the many activities that will be open to young people in the federal or state government. The first thing they will want to know is what education and/or training you have had. Nowadays the minimum, absolute minimum requirement for hundreds of jobs is two years' college, either at a four-year-college or at a junior college.

For another example: you have said that you don't expect to marry before

约翰·奥哈拉（John O'hara, 1905～1970年）

美国作家。他出生于宾夕法尼亚州的波特斯维尔，凭借处女作《相约萨马拉》一举成名。除在杂志发表一些短篇小说外，他一生共写了14部长篇小说，代表作有《向怒而生》《酒绿花红》及《北弗雷德里克街十号》等。其中《北弗雷德里克街十号》一书让他获得了美国国家图书奖。他的大部分小说以冷漠的且客观的笔触描写中上层阶级的道德观念和行为原则。

我亲爱的：

我一直在思考我们昨晚的谈话，而且我希望你也如此。

1962年，在某种程度上，是对威利·奥哈拉具有决定性的一年。你今年所做的某些决定将会对你今后几年可能想要做出的决定起到至关重要的作用。

譬如：假设当你20岁或21岁时，你会发现你想参加联邦政府或州政府为年轻人举办的某项活动。他们想要知道的第一件事就是你曾受过何种教育和／或培训。如今，对各行各业最低的，绝对最低的要求是两年的大学教育，要么在四年制大学里学习，要么在两年制大学里学习。

再譬如：你说过你不想在23岁以前结婚。好吧，那是你无法确定的事，但假设你的确等到23岁。假设你的未婚夫是个在某所大学里读研究

you are 23. Well, that is something you can't be sure of, but suppose you do wait till you're 23. Suppose your fianc¨?-husband is a young man who is taking graduate work at some university—law, medicine, the sciences, government work, etc.—and you and he are living in the vicinity of his graduate school. You may want to do work on the college or the graduate school level yourself, but I assure you will not be very enthusiastic about it if you have to start as a freshman of 23.

Now I could go on at some length, but the point I am aiming at it this: I want you to think very, very seriously about what you are going to do after St. Tim's. You are not Miss Rich bitch. You are not going to be Miss Church mouse, either, but you must think in terms of being able to earn at least part of your own living. I don't think you are going to fall in love with a dumb head. I think a dumb head, rich or not, would bore the hell out of you. Therefore it is extremely likely that the kind of boy you will like and fall in love with is going to be one who uses his brains to earn his living. That almost automatically means that he will be taking either graduate work or special post-college training of some sort. And even if you have children right away, you will want to keep up with him intellectually.

I can tell you from my own experience how important it is to have a wife with whom to discuss one's work. My first wife was a Wellesley B.A. and a Columbia M.A. and a diplomat, I think they are called, at the Sorbonne. Your mother did not go to college, but she could have. Sister and your mother both graduated from good schools and took courses at Columbia and your mother even attended lectures at Oxford without having to enroll there. Both your mother and Sister loved to read and read a great deal, and Sister is multilingual.

生的年轻人，他学的可能是法律、医学、理科、行政管理等等。你和他住在他攻读研究生的学校附近。你也许会希望你自己也上大学或读研究生。但我肯定，如果你不得不以一个 23 岁的新生身份开始，你将没有热情去学习。

现在我可以继续往下多说一些了，但我说这些的目的是：我希望你非常非常认真地思考从圣·蒂姆斯中学毕业后你将要做什么这一问题。你现在不是富家千金。你将来也不会是一贫如洗的姑娘，但你必须考虑你怎样才能起码挣到你自己的部分生活费。我想你不会爱上一个笨蛋。我认为，一个笨蛋，不管贫富与否，他都会让你极其厌烦的。因此，你将来喜欢或爱上的男孩极有可能是那种用自己的头脑来谋生的人。那自然而然地意味着，他将会读研究生或是接受大学毕业后的某种培训。此外，即使你想立即生孩子，你也会希望你们的孩子在才智方面能赶得上他。

我可以用我自己的经历告诉你，有一个能与自己讨论工作的妻子有多么重要。我的第一任妻子是威尔斯利大学的学士和哥伦比亚大学的硕士。我想，在索尔邦他们这些人被称为有文凭的人。你母亲没有上过大学，但她有能力上的。西斯特和你母亲都毕业于好的中学，并且在哥伦比亚大学修过课，而且你母亲甚至在不必注册的情况下，在牛津大学听过课。你母亲和西斯特都热爱读书，也读过大量的书，而且西斯特会说

Both your mother and Sister disliked women's colleges, but they did not dislike higher learning. They formed their dislike of college-girl types thirty years ago. The type has almost vanished, because the kind of girl your mother and Sister were then would be applying for college today. Everybody goes to college.

Now this is what's on my mind: the tentative program you have outlined for yourself does not seem to me very "realistic" in 1962 and 1963 and so on. I am hopeful that you will redirect yourself toward a good college so that you will get those two minimum-requirement years on your record and then be able, three years from now, to qualify for jobs or continue working for a degree. You will not regret having those two years on your record, whereas you might easily regret not having them. As your father, I have a duty to point these things out to you. But once I have done that I have to leave the real decision up to you.

Love,

Dad

多种语言。你母亲和西斯特都不喜欢女子大学，但她们并非不喜欢高等教育。她们对女大学生类型的不喜欢在三十年之前就成型了。这种类型现在已基本消失了，因为像当年你母亲和西斯特那样的女孩，如今都在申请读大学。每个人都去上大学。

现在我所考虑的是：你为自己所制定的暂时计划，在我看来这在1962 年或 1963 年或其他时候似乎都是不太现实的。我希望，你能重新为自己规划一下，去读一所好的大学，这样在你的履历上就会有受过两年大学教育的这一最低要求，三年之后，你就有资格找工作或继续学习并获得学位。你不会因为在你的履历上有这两年学习经历而后悔的；反而，你也许极易因为没有它们而懊悔。作为你的父亲，我有责任向你指明这些事情。但是，一旦我为你指明了这一切，我必须把真正的决定权留给你自己。

爱你的：爸爸
1962 年 1 月 7 日星期日
写于普林斯顿

## *Francis Fitzgerald to His Daughter*
## 弗朗西斯·菲茨杰拉德致女儿

Metro Goldwyn Mayer Corporation

Culver City, California

July 7, 1938

Dearest Scottie,

I don't think I will be writing letters many more years and I wish you would read this letter twice—bitter as it may seem. You will reject it now, but at a later period some of it may come back to you as truth. When I'm talking to you, you think of me as an older person, an "authority"; and when I speak of my own youth, what I say becomes unreal to you—for the young can't believe in the youth of their fathers. But perhaps this little bit will be understandable if I put it in writing.

When I was your age, I lived with a great dream. The dream grew and I learned how to speak of it and make people listen. Then the dream divided one day when I decided to marry your mother after all, even though I knew she was spoiled and meant no good to me. I was sorry immediately I had married her but, being patient in those days, made the best of it and got to love her

**名人小课堂**

弗朗西斯·菲茨杰拉德 (Francis Fitzgerald, 1896 ~ 1940)

出生于明尼苏达州圣保罗市，美国小说家，著名的编剧，也是"爵士时代"的发言人和"迷惘的一代"的代表作家之一。他的代表作品有《人间天堂》、《了不起的盖茨比》及《夜色温柔》等，他的小说生动地反映了 20 年代"美国梦"的破灭，展示了大萧条时期美国上层社会"荒原时代"的精神面貌。

亲爱的司各特：

我觉得我也没多少岁月可以给你写信了，我希望你能把这封信读上两遍——虽然这看上去比较痛苦。或许，你现在会抵制它，但是不久之后，信里的某些内容将成为你的真理。当我在跟你说这些的时候，你觉得我已是一个老人，是个"专横"的人；当我向你讲述我自己年轻时的经历，我所说的一切对你来说是不真实的——因为年轻人总是不相信父辈们年轻时候的事情。但是，如果我能把它写下来的话，你也许会好理解一点。

当我像你那么大的时候，我有一个伟大的梦想。梦想在成长，我也学会了如何去阐述它，让别人聆听它。有一天，梦想破碎了，那就是当我最终决定和你妈妈结婚的时候，尽管我知道她从小娇生惯养，而且对我也无好处。娶了她之后，我就立刻后悔了，但是那些日子我一直很耐心，尽量做到最好以维持我们的婚姻关系，通过另一种方式去爱她。随着你的到来，有很长一段时间，我们的生活充满了幸福。但我是一个分

in another way. You came along and for a long time we made quite a lot of happiness out of our lives. But I was a man divided—she wanted me to work too much for her and not enough for my dream. She realized too late that work was dignity, and the only dignity, and tried to atone for it by working herself, but it was too late and she broke and is broken forever.

It was too late also for me to recoup the damage—I had spent most of my resources, spirit and material, on her, but I struggled on for five years till my health collapsed, and all I cared about was drink and forgetting.

The mistake I made was marrying her. We belonged to different worlds—she might have been happy with a kind simple man in a southern garden. She didn't have the strength for the big stage—sometimes she pretended, and pretended beautifully, but she didn't have it. She was soft when she should have been hard, and hard when she should have been yielding. She never knew how to use her energy—she's passed that failing on to you.

For a long time I hated her mother for giving her nothing in the line of good habit—nothing but "getting by" and conceit. I never wanted to see again in this world women who were brought up as idlers. And one of my chief desires in life was to keep you from being that kind of person, one who brings ruin to themselves and others. When you began to show disturbing signs at about fourteen, I comforted myself with the idea that you were too precocious socially and a strict school would fix things. But sometimes I think that idlers seem to be a special class for whom nothing can be planned, plead as one will with them—their only contribution to the human family is to warm a seat at the common table.

裂的人——她想要我为她做太多的工作，因而我没有足够的精力与时间去追求自己的梦想。当她意识到工作就是尊严，而且是唯一的尊严，一切都为时已晚了。她还试图通过自己的工作来弥补这些，但是已经太迟了，她的身体已经不行了，彻底地不行了。

弥补所受的伤害，对我来说也为时已晚了——我已经将自己绝大部分的资源、精力和财富都倾注在她的身上了，但是我依旧奋斗了5年，直到我的身体也垮掉了，而现在我所关心的事情只有借酒消愁。

我所犯的错误就是和她结婚。我与她属于不同的世界——假如她和南方的庄园里的一个善良单纯的男人结婚的话，她可能会过得很快乐。她没有适应大舞台的能力——有时她会假装有这个能力，而且装得很好，但事实上她并没有。在应该强硬的时候，她表现得软弱；在应该屈服的时候，她却表现得很强硬。她从来都不知道如何运用自己的力量——她已经把这些缺点都传给了你。

有很长一段时间，我恨她的母亲没有教给她任何好的习惯——除了"得过且过"和狂妄自负。在这个世界上，我永远不想再见到任何一个女人被养育成一个游手好闲者。我生命中主要的心愿之一就是让你不要变成那种人，那种给自己和别人都带来毁灭的人。你14岁时开始显露出令人烦扰的迹象，那时我安慰自己说，你可能在社交方面早熟了一些，接受严格的学校教育将会解决这些问题。但是，有时我也这样想，那些游手好闲的人似乎是一个特殊的阶层，对他们来说，没有什么事情是可以被计划的，他们会以此为自己辩护——他们对于人类家庭惟一的贡献，就是占据一张普通桌子前的一个座位罢了。

My reforming days are over, and if you are that way I don't want to change you. But I don't want to be upset by idlers inside my family or out. I want my energies and my earnings for people who talk my language.

I have begun to fear that you don't. You don't realize that what I am doing here is the last tired effort of a man who once did something finer and better. There is not enough energy, or call it money, to carry anyone who is dead weight and I am angry and resentful in my soul when I feel that I am doing this. People like—and your mother must be carried because their illness makes them useless. But it is a different story that you have spent two years doing no useful work at all, improving neither your body nor your mind, but only writing reams and reams of dreary letters to dreary people, with no possible object except obtaining invitations which you could not accept. Those letters go on, even in your sleep, so that I know your whole trip now is one long waiting for the post. It is like an old gossip that cannot still her tongue.

You have reached the age when one is of interest to an adult only insofar as one seems to have a future. The mind of a little child is fascinating, for it looks on old things with new eyes—but at about twelve this change. The adolescent offers nothing, can do nothing, say nothing that the adult cannot do better. Living with you in Baltimore (and you have told Harold that I alternated between strictness and neglect, by which I suppose you mean the times I was so inconsiderate as to have T. B. o or to retire into myself to write, for I had little social life apart from you) represented a rather too domestic duty forced on me by your mother's illness. But I endured your Top Hats and Telephones until the day you snubbed me at dancing school, less willingly after that...

世界上最感人的书信
The Most Inspiring Letters In the World

我重新自我调整的日子已经结束了，假如你选择那种游手好闲的生活方式，我也不想去改变你。但是，不管是在家里还是在外面，我都不想被游手好闲的人烦扰。我希望自己的精力和收入能花在那些与我有共同语言的人们身上。

我开始担心你并没有意识到这些，没有意识到我在这里所做的一切，是一个曾经做出优秀业绩的人最后的疲倦的努力。我已经没有足够的精力，或者说足够的金钱来支持任何一个纯粹是沉重的负担的人。而当我感觉自己正在做这些的时候，我内心充满愤怒和怨恨。像你妈妈那样的人必须得到支持，因为他们的病痛致使他们无所作为。但是，你的事情就另当别论了：你已经度过了两年碌碌无为的生活，你既没有改进你的身体状况，也没有充实你的头脑知识，你惟一做的就是给那些沉闷的人们一封接一封地写沉闷的信件，除了收到一些你自己并不接受的邀请之外，你做这件事没有任何目的。甚至在睡觉的时候，那些信件都在继续。因此，我知道你现在的整个旅程就是一个等待邮件的漫长过程。它就像一个爱嚼舌的老妇无法令她的舌头安分下来一样。

你已经到了这样的年龄：只有当你看起来有前途时，大人们才会对你产生兴趣。小孩子的心灵是迷人的，因为儿童用全新的眼睛看待旧的事物——但是大约 12 岁的时候，这种情形就改变了。青少年们提供不了任何东西，他们什么也不会做，什么也不会说，而成年人对那些事却可以做得更好。由于你母亲的病情，强加在我身上的一点家庭责任的体现就是要和你一起住在巴尔的摩。（你曾跟哈罗德说我对你的态度在严格和疏忽之间交替变化，据此我猜你的意思是指当年我因为过于轻率而感染了肺结核；或者是我只顾自己一心写作，因为除了你之外，我几乎没有任何社交活动）。但是，我对你戴大礼帽和打电话的行为，一直都忍耐，

To sum up: what you have done to please me or make me proud is practically negligible since the time you made yourself a good diver at camp (and now you are softer than you have ever been). In your career as a "wild society girl", vintage of 1925, I'm not interested. I don't want any of it— it would bore me, like dining with the Ritz Brothers. When I do not feel you are "going somewhere", your company tends to depress me for the silly waste and triviality involved. On the other hand, when occasionally I see signs of life and intention in you, there is no company in the world I prefer. For there is no doubt that you have something in your belly, some real gusto for life—a real dream of your own—and my idea was to wed it to something solid before it was too late—as it was too late for your mother to learn anything when she got around to it. Once when you spoke French as a child it was enchanting with your odd bits of knowledge—now your conversation is as commonplace as if you'd spent the last two years in the Corn Hollow High School—what you saw in Life and read in Sexy Romances.

I shall come East in September to meet your boat—but this letter is a declaration that I am no longer interested in your promissory notes but only in what I see. I love you always but I am only interested by people who think and work as I do and it isn't likely that I shall change at my age. Whether you will—or want to—remains to be seen.

Daddy


P. S. If you keep the diary, please don't let it be the dry stuff I could buy in a ten franc guide book. I'm not interested in dates and places, even the Battle

世界上最感人的书信
The Most Moving Letters In the World

直到那天在舞蹈学校你冷落我，从那以后，我才稍微不乐意……

总而言之，自从你在夏令营把自己训练成一个优秀的潜水员，之后（你现在已经比以前退步了不少），你所做的能让我高兴和自豪的事情事实上几乎可以忽略不计。你作为"野蛮社会女孩"的经历，那是在1925年，我一点儿也不感兴趣。我不想知道任何关于它的事情——它会令我心烦意乱，就像跟里兹兄弟共进晚餐一样。当我感觉不到你在进步的时候，你的陪伴存在令我有沮丧的倾向，因为那是愚蠢的浪费和琐事。从另一面来说，当我偶然看到你身上散发出生活的气息和向上的意志时，我在世界上将不再需要任何陪伴。因为毫无疑问，你身上依然存在某些东西，一种对于生活的真正热忱——一种属于你自己的真正的梦想——我的想法是在还来得及之前，把它跟一些可靠实在的事物捆绑在一起——因为当你妈妈开始考虑去学些什么的时候，却为时已晚了。当你还是个孩子时，你曾学过说法语，你对知识的零星掌握让人着迷——而现在你的谈话却非常平庸，似乎过去两年你是在考恩·霍洛高级中学度过的——就像你在《生活》和《性感传奇》中所看到的内容那样。

9月份，我将到东部去接你——但是，这封信是一个声明：我将不再对你的许诺感兴趣，只对自己亲眼所见的感兴趣。我会一直爱你，但让我感兴趣的只是那些与我志同道合的人，而且到我这样的年纪，我也不可能做出什么样的改变。无论你是否愿意——或者是想要——拭目以待吧。

爸爸

又及：如果你还坚持写日记的话，请不要让你的日记成为干瘪瘪的东西，那些内容在我用10法郎就能买到的指南书里就有。我对日期、地

of New Orleans, unless you have some unusual reaction to them. Don't try to be witty in the writing, unless it's natural—just true and real.

P. P. S. Will you please read this letter a second time? I wrote it over twice.

名，甚至"新奥尔良战役"都不感兴趣，除非你对它们有一些与众不同的反应。写作时，不要试图追求措辞巧妙诙谐，除非是自然而然的——只需要准确真实。

　　再及：你愿意把这封信再看一遍吗？这封信我写了不止两遍。


1938 年 7 月 7 日

写于加利福尼亚州，科佛市

米高梅电影公司

## Chapter 4

# 有一种交流受益一生

*The distance a person can reach depends on who counterparts; How good a person is depends on who gives him the directions; How successful a man is depends on who accompanies him.*

一个人能走多远，要看他有谁同行；一个人有多优秀，要看他有谁指点；一个人有多成功，要看他有谁相伴。

# 本杰明·富兰克林致姐姐

## （简·梅科姆太太）

London, September16, 1758

Dear Sister,

I received your favor of June 17. I wonder you have had no letter from me since my being in England. I have written you at least two, and I think a third before this, and what was next to waiting on you in person, sent you my picture. In June last I sent Benny a trunk of books, and wrote to him; I hope they have come to hand, and that he meets with encouragement in his business. I congratulate you on the conquest of Cape Breton, and hope as your people took it by praying, the first time, you will now pray that it may never be given up again, which you then forgot. Billy is well, but in the country. I left him at Tunbridge Wells, where we spent a fortnight, and he is now gone with some company to see Portsmouth. We have been together over a great part of England this summer and among other places, visited the town our father was born in, and found some relations in that part of the country still living.

Our cousin Jane Franklin, daughter of our uncle John, died about a year ago. We saw her husband, Robert Page, who gave us some old letters to his

名人小课堂

本杰明·富兰克林（Benjamin Franklin, 1706 ～ 1790 年）

美国著名的政治家、社会活动家、科学家、发明家。他出生于波士顿一个工人家庭，由于家境贫寒，只上了两年学就辍学当了学徒，12 岁时到他大哥的印刷所里当学徒，长期从事印刷工作，同时刻苦自学。他曾化名投稿，报纸编辑以为文章"出自名家手笔"。作为政治家，在美国和世界历史上，他与许多重要事件有关。他在北美独立战争中起了重大作用，是美国的创建人之一，参与起草了《独立宣言》和美国宪法。

亲爱的姐姐：

我已收到你 6 月 17 日的来信。我怀疑自我到英格兰后，你再也没有收到我的任何信。但是我至少给你写过两封，而且在这封信之前还有第三封，在等待你本人的期间，紧接着我又给你寄去了我的照片。最近的，6 月份我还给本尼寄去了一箱书，也给他写了一封信；我希望他悉数收到，并希望他工作中受到鼓励。祝贺你征服了布里敦角，希望正如你的人民第一次通过祈祷得到了它一样，现在你们将祈祷它永远不会再次被丢弃，那时你们已将它忘记。比利很好，现在住在乡下。我把他留在了滕布里奇韦尔斯，我们在那呆了两周，现在他又与别人结伴去参观朴次茅斯了。这个夏天，我们一起游览了英格兰的大部分地区，其中，我们还参观了我们的父亲出生的小镇，并找到了一些在那个地区仍然健在的亲戚们。

wife, from Uncle Benjamin. In one of them, dated Boston, July 4, 1723, he writes that your uncle Josiah has a daughter Jane, about twelve years old, a good-humored child. So keep up to your character, and don't be angry when you have no letters. In a little book he sent her, called "None but Christ," he wrote an acrostick on her name, which for namesake's sake, as well as the good advice it contains, I transcribe and send you.

"Illuminated from on high,

And shining brightly in your sphere.

Ne'er faint, but keep a steady eye,

Expecting endless pleasures there."

"Flee vice as you'd a serpent flee;

Raise faith and hope three stories higher,

And let Christ's endless love to thee

Ne'er cease to make thy love aspire.

Kindness of heart by words express,

Let your obedience be sincere,

In prayer and praise you God address,

Nor cease, till he can cease to hear. "

After professing truly that I had a great esteem and veneration for the pious author, permit me a little to play the commentator and critic on these lines. The meaning of three stories higher seems somewhat obscure. You are to understand, then, that faith, hope, and charity have been called the three steps of Jacob's ladder, reaching from earth to heaven; our author calls them stories, likening religion to a building, and these are the three stories of the Christian edifice. Thus improvement in religion is called building up and edification.

我们的堂妹简·富兰克林，约翰叔叔的女儿，一年前去世了。我们见到了她的丈夫罗伯特·佩奇，他给了我们一些本杰明叔叔写给他妻子的旧信。在其中一封 1723 年 7 月 4 日写于波土顿的信中，他写到你们的叔叔乔赛亚有一个女儿名叫简，大约 12 岁，是一个脾气很好的孩子。因此请你保持这种性格，没有收到信也不要生气。在叔叔送给她的一本书名为《独一无二的耶稣》的薄书里，他以她的名义写了一首离合体诗。现在我把它抄写下来并寄给你，不仅因为你与她同名的缘故，而且因为其中包含的忠告。

"高高地照亮着，

在你的领地上闪闪发亮。

不要眩晕，只要保持坚定的目光，

期待那里无尽的欢乐。"

"邪恶逃走了，就如同你驱走了恶魔；

把信仰和希望再提高三层楼，

让耶稣赐予你无尽的爱

从不停止你对爱的渴望。

去用语言表达心灵美，

让你的顺从成为一种真诚，

在祈祷中，赞美上帝的话语，

不要停止，直到上帝停止聆听。"

坦诚地说，我对虔诚的作者怀着无限的尊重和敬佩，请允许我给这几行诗做一点注释和评论。"再提高三层楼"，其意似乎有点模糊不清。不过，你知道人们一直把忠诚、希望和慈悲称作雅各布天梯的三级台阶，从地球通往天堂；我们的作者把宗教比喻成楼房，于是把三级台阶称之为三层楼，而忠诚、希望和慈悲就是基督教圣殿的三层楼。因此宗教的

Faith is then the ground floor, hope is up one pair of stairs. My dear beloved Jenny, don't delight so much to dwell in those lower rooms, but get as fast as you can into the garret, for in truth the best room in the house is charity. For my part, I wish the house was turned upside down; 'tis so difficult (when one is fat) to go upstairs; and not only so, but I imagine hope and faith may be more firmly built upon charity, than charity upon faith and hope. However that may be, I think it the better reading to say—

"Raise faith and hope one story higher."

Correct it boldly, and I'll support the alteration; for, when you are up two stories already, if you raise your building three stories higher you will make five in all, which is two more than there should be, you expose your upper rooms more to the winds and storms. And, besides, I am afraid the foundation will hardly bear them, unless indeed you build with such light stuff as straw and stubble, and that, you know, won't stand fire. Again, where the author says,

"Kindness of heart by words express,"

Strike out words, and put in deeds. The world is too full of compliments already. They are the rank growth of every soil, and choke the good plants of benevolence, and beneficence; nor do I pretend to be the first in this comparison of words and actions to plants; you may remember an ancient poet, whose works we have all studied and copied at school long ago.

"A man of words and not of deeds

Is like a garden full of weeds."

It is a pity that good works, among some sorts of people, are so little valued, and good words admired in their stead: I mean seemingly pious discourses, instead of humane benevolent actions. Those they almost put out

升华就是渐进和顿悟。忠诚便是第一层，希望是第二层。我亲爱的詹妮，不要太高兴于停留在那些低楼层的房间里，而要尽你所能地迅速到达顶楼，因为事实上房子里最好的房间是慈悲。在我看来，我倒希望整个房子完全倒置过来，因为上楼梯太难了（当一个人太胖时），不仅如此，我想象着希望与忠诚建立在慈悲之上较之于慈悲建立在忠诚与希望之上会更牢固。无论怎样，我想这样说妥当一些——

"把忠诚与希望提高一层。"

大胆地改正它，而且我会支持这个修改的；因为当你已上了两层楼时，如果你把你的楼房增高三层，总共就造了五层，比应该有的多了两层，这样上面的房间则更多地暴露于风雨之中；除此之外，恐怕地基也难以承受，除非你真的是用那些很轻的材料诸如稻草和头发去建造，但你知道那是经不住考验的。另外，作者说，

"用语言表达心灵美，"

删去"语言"一词，换上"行为"。这个世界已经充满了太多恭维，这些恭维在每一块土地上犹如杂草丛生，从而抑制了慈善和德行这样的好植物的生长。我并没有自命是第一个把言语和行为比作植物的人；你或许记得一位古代诗人，很久以前在学校里，我们都读过并抄录过他的作品。

"一个只说不做的人

就像是长满杂草的花园。"

很遗憾，一些慈善行为在某些人群中是如此没有价值，相反一些华丽辞藻却受到了他们的赞美：我指的是那些貌似虔诚的演讲，而不是人类的仁慈行为。几乎令人局促不安的是，那些人称道德为腐败的道德，

of countenance, by calling morality rotten morality, righteousness ragged righteousness, and even filthy rags—and when you mention virtue, pucker up their noses as if they smelt a stink; at the same time that they eagerly snuff up an empty canting harangue, as if it was a pose of the choicest flowers. So they have inverted the good old verse, and say now

"A man of deeds and not of words

Is like a garden full of—"

I have forgot the rhyme, but remember 'tis something the very reverse of perfume. So much by way of commentary.

My wife will let you see my letter, containing an account of our travels, which I would have you read to sister Dowse, and give my love to her. I have no thoughts of returning till next year, and then may possibly have the pleasure of seeing you and yours. Taking Boston in my way home. My love to brother and all your children, concludes at this time from, dear Jenny, your affectionate brother.

B.FRANKLIN

正直为褴褛的正直，甚至是充满了污秽的褴褛——而一提到美德，他们就好像嗅到了一股臭味似的，皱起他们的鼻子；与此同时，他们渴望地嗅着伪善的高谈阔论，仿佛那是一束最好的花环。因此，他们把好的古诗前后颠倒，改写成：

"一个只做而不说的人

就像是花园长满了——"

我已忘记那句尾的韵脚，但记得那绝对不是什么好话。评述就这么多。

我妻子会给你看我的信，里面包含了我们旅行的记叙，希望你把信读给道斯妹妹听，代我向她问好。我想明年才回来，那时可能有幸见到你和你们一家。我在返家途中将取道波士顿。向哥哥和你的所有的孩子问好。亲爱的詹妮，我就此搁笔，爱你的弟弟。

本·富兰克林

1758 年 9 月 16 日

写于伦敦

# *Thomas Jefferson to His Nephew*
## 托马斯·杰弗逊致侄儿

Paris, August10, 1787

Dear Peter,—I have received your two letters of December the 30th and April the 18th, and am very happy to find by them, as well as by letters from Mr. Wythe, that you have been so fortunate as to attract his notice and good will; I am sure you will find this to have been one of the most fortunate events of your life, as I have ever been sensible it was of mine. I enclose you a sketch reading, which submit to his correction. Many of these are among your father's books, which you should have brought to you. As I do not recollect those of them not in his library, you must write to me for them, making out a catalogue of such as you think you shall have occasion for, in eighteen months from the date of your letter, and consulting Mr. Wythe on the subject to this sketch. I will add a few particular observations:

Italian. I fear that learning this language will confound you French and Spanish. Being all of them degenerated dialects of the Latin, they are apt to mix in conversation. I have never seen a person speaking the three languages, who did not mix them. It is a delightful language, but late events having rendered the Spanish more useful, lay it aside to prosecute that.

名人小课堂

托马斯·杰斐逊 (Thomas Jefferson, 1743 ~ 1826 年)

美国政治家、思想家、哲学家、科学家、教育家，第三任美国总统。他是美国独立战争期间的主要领导人之一，《独立宣言》的主要起草人。他在任期间，向法国购买了路易斯安那州，使美国领土近乎增加了一倍。他被普遍视为美国历史上最杰出的总统之一，同华盛顿、林肯和罗斯福齐名。

亲爱的彼得：

你写于 12 月 30 日和 4 月 18 日的两封来信我已收到。从你的两封信件以及威思先生来信的内容中得知，你已经很幸运地引起了威思先生的注意并获得了他的好感，对此我表示非常高兴。我相信你会发现这将是你生活中最幸运的事情之一，正如我曾经一直意识到的一样，那也是我的最幸运的事情。在此，我附上一份概要读本，并将此提交给威思先生进行修正。其中许多书都在你父亲的藏书中，你应该都已随身带去。由于我已想不起来具体哪些书是你父亲的书房中没有的，所以你一定要将你认为从你写信的那天起至今后的 18 个月内有机会接触到的所有的书列一个清单出来，然后就此清单内容详细地咨询威思先生，确定好后写信告诉我。关于这个概要，我还要特别地补充几点个人看法：

意大利语。我担心学习意大利语会使你把法语和西班牙语与之混淆不清。毕竟这几种语言都是由拉丁语退化衍生出来的方言，所以在会话的应用中它们是比较容易混淆的。我还从未见过一个人同时说这三种语言而没将它们混淆的。意大利语是一门令人愉快的语言，但是近期发生的事件说明西班牙语更为实用，所以你还是先将这个事情搁置一边吧。

道德哲学。我认为听这门课的讲座纯属浪费时间。假如有人把我们

Moral Philosophy. I think it lost time to attend lectures on this branch. He who made us would have been a pitiful bungler, if he had made the rules of our moral conduct a matter of science. For one man of science, there are thousands who are not. What would have become of them? Man was destined for society. His morality, therefore, was to be formed to this object. He was endowed with a sense of right and wrong, merely relative to this. This sense is as much a part of his nature, as the sense of hearing, seeing, feeling; It is the true foundation of morality, and not the tokaol, truth, etc., as fanciful writers have imagined. The moral sense, or conscience, is as much a part of man as his leg or arm. It is given to all human beings in a stronger or weaker degree, as force of members is given them in a greater or less degree. It may be strengthened by exercise, as may any particular limb of the body. This sense is submitted, indeed, in some degree, to the guidance of reason; but it is a small stock which is required for this even a less one than what we call common sense. State a moral case to a plowman and a professor. The former will decide it as well and often better than the latter, because he has not been led astray by artificial rules. In this branch, therefore, read good books, because they will encourage, as well as direct your feelings. The writings of Sterne, particularly, form the best course of morality that ever was written. Besides these, read the books mentioned in the enclosed paper, and, above all things, lose no occasion of exercising your dispositions to be grateful, to be generous, to be charitable, to be humane, to be true, just, firm, orderly, courageous, etc.. Consider every act of this kind, as an exercise which will strengthen your moral faculties and increase your worth.

Traveling. This makes men wiser, but less happy. When men of sober age travel, they gather knowledge, which they may apply usefully for their

的道德行为准则定为一门科学，并要求我们去听课，那么那个人一定是一个可怜的蠢蛋。对于一个科学家来说，世上会有成千上万的人不是。他们将会是怎样的呢？人是具有社会属性的人，因此，人的道德也是在社会中形成的。人与生俱来拥有与此相关的判断是非的能力，这种能力就像听、说、感觉等一样是人类本能的一部分；它是道德真正的基础，而不是如那些富于幻想的作家所想象的那样是美、真等的基础。道德观念，或者说良心，就像一个人的腿或胳膊一样，是他身体的一部分。人类被赋予的道德观念程度不一样，有强也有弱，就好像人类被赋予的力量也有大有小一样。道德观念就像身体的任何一个肢体一样，可以通过锻炼来得到加强。在某种程度上，道德观念实际上的确服从于推理的向导，但服从于推理向导的道德观念只是很小的一部分，甚至比我们的常识还要少。向一个农民和一个教授讲述一宗道德案件，两者都会做出判断，而且前者还经常比后者判定得要好，因为他没有被人为制定的清规戒律引入歧途。因此，在道德哲学这一学科，你要做的就是多读好书，因为它们不但能鼓励你，而且能引导你的感觉，尤其是斯特恩的书，它们是已有的道德教科书中最好的教程。除此以外，还要读我在附件中提到的那些书；最重要的是，不可错失任何一个可以陶冶情操的机会，待人方面要做到：永怀感恩之心、宽宏大度、友善仁慈；处事方面要做到：尊重事实、公正合理、坚定有条理、勇敢等等。把这其中的每一个方面的实践活动都看作是一个可以增强你的道德观念以及提升自我价值的锻炼。

旅游。旅游使人越来越聪明，但人们从中得到的快乐却越来越少。不惑之年的中年人旅游，可以获取知识，并可能运用这些知识为他们的

country; but they are subject ever after to recollections mixed with regret; their affections are weakened by being extended over more objects; and they learn new habits which cannot be gratified when they return home. Young men, who travel, are exposed to all these inconveniences in a higher degree, to others still more serious, and do not acquire that wisdom for which a previous foundation is requisite by repeated and just observations at home. The glare of pomp and pleasure is analogous to the motion of the blood; it absorbs all their affection and attention, they are torn from it as from the only good in this world, and return to their home as to a place of exile and condemnation. Their eyes are forever turned back to the object they have lost, and its recollection poisons the residue of their lives. Their first and most delicate passions are hackneyed on unworthy objects here, and they carry home the dregs, insufficient to make themselves or anybody else happy. Add to this, that a habit of idleness, an inability to apply themselves to business is acquired, and renders them useless to themselves and their country. These observations are founded in experience. There is no place where your pursuit of knowledge will be so little obstructed by foreign objects, as in your own country, nor any, wherein the virtues of the heart will be less exposed to be weakened. Be good, be learned, and be industrious, and you will not want the aid of traveling, to render you precious to your country, dear to your friends, happy within yourself. I repeat my advice, to take a great deal of exercise, and on foot. Health is the first requisite after morality. Write to me often, and be assured of the interest I take in your success, as well as the warmth of those sentiments of attachment with which I am, dear Peter, your affectionate friend.

国家服务。但是过后，他们却摆脱不了夹杂着遗憾的回忆之苦；他们的情感会因投入到过多的事物上而减弱；他们还可以学到一些新习惯，但当返回到自己的祖国时，却对那些新习惯并不感到欣慰。豆蔻年华的年轻人旅游，更容易遭遇到所有的这些麻烦以及其他更为严重的问题。他们不具备足够的见识，因为这些见识的形成需要有一定的基础，而这个基础只有通过在家里通过反复和客观的观察才能建立。浮华和快乐的光芒就好比血液的运动。它吸引了他们所有的情感和关注，要从中抽身分离，就像是要与世上唯一的好东西分开一样；当他们返回家乡时，就好像回到了一个流放和服刑之地。他们的眼睛永远盯在他们已经失去的东西上面，其回忆毒害了他们的余生。他们最最重要的激情在这里被毫无价值的事物消耗殆尽，他们把糟粕带回家，到头来既没让自己开心，还惹得别人不高兴。此外，他们养成了懒散的习气，丧失了干事业的能力，这使得他们既无助于自己，也无助于国家。这些观察到的现象在过去的一些经验中可以被发现。在这个世界上，当你追求学习知识的时候，在哪都不如在自己的国家那样极少受到外物的阻碍；在哪都不如在自己的国家那样对自己的心灵的美德产生极弱的影响。做人要有教养，要有学问，要勤奋，那样你将不再需要通过旅游的帮助来使自己变得于国家宝贵，于朋友亲切，于自我快乐。我重申我的忠告，多运动，多步行。健康是继德行之后，人类最必不可少的东西。记得常给我写信，并请确信我对你的成功总是充满兴趣、对其所附属的那些情感总是充满着热情。亲爱的彼得，你挚爱的朋友。

1787 年 8 月 10 日

写于巴黎

# Margaret Fuller to Her Brother (Arthur B. Fuller)

## 玛格丽特·富勒致弟弟
### （阿瑟·B·富勒）

Jamaica Plain

20th, December 1840

It is not, my dear Arthur, because I "have so little to say to you" that my letters are short, but because bad health and many engagements oblige me to such economy of time. You know, too, that writing is of all occupations, the very worst for my malady, and as I must do a great deal at any rate I abstain always when I can. Bear this in mind, and don't measure my interest in your pursuits, or affection for yourself by the number or length of my letters.

I continue to manage very well. The fatted pig is killed, and was found in good order' not—withstanding your and Richard's evil omens from the character of our prodigal son here. We banquet on pork rather more constantly than is agreeable to a "true believer" like myself.

My other life continues its usual course. I have been to hear the Sonnambula, but with scarce more satisfaction than our fastidious Richard derived from his concert, of which, I suppose, he has given you an account.

玛格丽特·富勒（Margaret Fuller, 1810 ~ 1850 年）

美国作家、评论家、社会改革家、早期女权运动领袖。她出生在马萨诸塞州的坎布里奇港，从小受父亲的教育影响。她是新英格兰先验论派的著名成员，1840 ~ 1842 年，即杂志发行的前两年，她负责先验论杂志《日晷》（The Dial）的编辑工作。

我亲爱的亚瑟：

并不是因为我"对你无话可说"，我的信才那么短，而是因为我糟糕的健康状况以及繁多的事务迫使我不得不节约时间。你也知道，在我所有的工作中，写作对我的病是最为不利的。而且，因为我无论如何都得做许多事，所以我就尽量避免去做我可以避免的事。你要记住这一点，不要用我的信的多少和长短去衡量我对你的追求的兴趣、或对你的感情。

我一切仍然安排得很好。长膘的猪已经杀了，一切都有条不紊，也并没有因我们在这扮演了忏悔的罪人而应验了你和理查德所预示的凶兆。我们经常举办猪肉宴会，而这对像我这样的"忠实信徒"来说是不相符的。

我生活的其他方面一如既往。我曾去听过《梦游女》，但我对这场音乐会的满意度并不比我们爱挑剔的理查德对他所听的音乐会的满意度好多少。我估计，他给你描述过那场音乐会。

The news of Ellen's illness was sad to me both on her account and Mother's over whose visit a cloud is cast at once. Mr. Keats's letter to me was kind and clear. She will have, I am sure, all the attention and wise counsel she needs. The fever was gone and only a rheumatic affection remained of which the physician thought she would soon be free. I shall hope very soon to hear again.

About your school I do not think I can give you much advice which would be of value unless I knew your position more in detail. The important rule is, as in all relations with our fellow creatures, never forget that, if they are imperfect persons, they are immortal souls, and treat them as you would wish to be treated by the light of that though.

As to the application of means—Abstain from punishment as much as possible and use encouragement as far as you can without flattery. But be even more careful as to strict truth in this regard towards children than to persons of your own age. For to the child the parent or teacher is the representative of Justice, and as that of life is severe, an education which in any degree, excites vanity is the very worst preparation for that general and crowded school.

I doubt not you will teach grammar well, as I saw you aimed at principles in your practice —In geography, try to make pictures of the scenes, that they may be present to their imagination, and the nobler faculties be brought into action as well as memory—In history study and try to paint the characters of great men; they best interpret the leadings of events amid the nations.

I am pleased with your way of speaking of both people and pupils, your view seems from the right point, yet beware of over great pleasure in

埃伦生病的消息让我感到很难过，既因为她的缘故，也因为母亲的缘故，因为母亲看过她之后，立即心情乌云密布。济慈先生给我的来信既亲切又明了。我肯定她将得到她所需要的一切关心和明智的忠告。她已经退烧，只是风湿病后遗症还没有治好，医生原本说她会很快康复的。我希望尽快听到她的消息。

对于你的教学，我无法给你多少有价值的建议，除非我对你的现状有更加详细的了解。与我们人类相关的重要原则是，永远不要忘记，即使人们不完美，他们也是不朽的灵魂。有鉴于此，你若希望别人如何对待你，你就应该如何去对待别人。

至于使用什么方法——尽量避免使用惩罚，尽可能使用鼓励的方式，但不要奉承他们。对孩子要比对你的同龄人更加注意坚持真理。因为对孩子来说，父母或老师就是公正的代表；而且，因为生活是艰辛的，所以任何层次的教育若引起孩子的虚荣心理，那对于普通的众多学校来说是极其糟糕的。

我毫不怀疑你能教好语法，因为我看到你在实习时重点针对语法规则。在地理课中，尽量制作些场景图片，这可供他们想象，并把这种较好的视觉官能带入行为和记忆之中。在历史课中，尝试描绘出伟人们的性格；它们最能说明这些人在各国的重大事件中所起的领导作用。

我很喜欢你谈论他人和学生的方式，你貌似从正确的角度发表观点，

being popular or even beloved. As far as an amiable disposition and powers of entertainment make you so, it is a happiness, but is there one grain of plausibility, it is poison. —But I will not play Mentor much, lest I make you averse to write to your very affectionate sister.

Margaret

但是你要谨防因受欢迎甚至被人爱戴而过分沾沾自喜。至于你的和蔼可亲的性情和快乐的性格使你如此，这是一种幸福，但你略有点儿花言巧语，这是有害的。但我不多跟你说教了，以免使你不乐意给你亲爱的姐姐写信了。

玛格丽特

1840 年 12 月 20 日

写于牙买加平原

*Virgil Thomson to His Sister*
*(Ruby Gleason)*

# 弗吉尔·汤姆森致姐姐
## （鲁比·格利森）

Cambridge

August 26, 1920

Dear Sister,

The news of the stork's visit is the most excitement I have had yet. It is exactly what I had hoped would happen for a long time, because I think a child in the family will do us all good. Of course it's difficult and expensive and dangerous, but we mustn't be afraid of things like that. A family that doesn't go through them and risk things is decayed. There is no way of protecting ourselves from life that isn't stupid, and the only way to be somebody is to do all the important things and do them with gusto. To get married without having children is rather begging the question, I think, side-stepping the main issue. I am glad the family isn't decaying, and I hope when you can afford it there will be one or two more. I hope it is a squalling lusty boy with dark red hair and freckles.

If the others weren't pleased at the prospect, it was clumsy not to say so.

名人小课堂

弗吉尔·汤姆森（Virgil Thomson, 1896～1989 年）

美国作曲家、音乐评论家。他出生于密苏里州堪萨斯城，毕业于哈佛大学，1940 年回到纽约定居。1954 年担任纽约《先驱论坛报》乐评人期间，极大促进了人们对当代音乐的接受能力，促使歌剧、音乐会提高演出水准。他在英文歌剧谱曲方面颇具才华，代表作品有：《三幕剧中的四圣徒》、《拜伦勋爵》及《我们大家的母亲》等。

亲爱的姐姐：

婴儿即将诞生的消息，是我所听到的最令我感到兴奋的事情。这正是我长期以来所盼望的事情，因为我认为家里有个小孩对我们大家都有好处。当然，生孩子既辛苦又费钱，而且还危险，但我们不能害怕那样的事情。一个经不起事、不敢冒险的家族是衰败的家族。我们无法让自己远离并不乏味的生活，唯一能使我们成为重要人物的方法，就是去做所有重要的事情，并且带着兴致去做。我认为，结婚而不要孩子是回避问题的实质，也就是回避主要问题。我为咱们的家族没有正在走向衰败而感到高兴。我希望，若你们能养得起的话，可以再多要一个或两个孩子。我希望即将出生的这个孩子是一个长着深红色头发和雀斑，会哇哇大哭且精力充沛的男孩。

如果其他的人对孩子的出生感到不高兴，他们不说出来是很愚蠢的。

But I suppose we are nothing if not frank in the family. Mother has always had the idea that there was something a bit vulgar about having a baby, as if the best people didn't do it, whereas the "best people" are exactly the ones who still have families of eight and ten, while the middle classes nowadays are getting selfish and timorous and either have no children at all or else devote themselves to one spoiled baby. I'll bet Roy is glad.

By the way, you must not let the family in, be sure and go out every day to exercise, clear up till the confinement, and go in the motor all you can. Also please don't economize. I insist on your going to a hospital and having a nurse for the first few months. Anything else is not safe.

Please tell the family they deserve a good spanking for not wanting to tell me (which would have been outrageous) and for being selfish and stupid in their attitude.

If you are not too busy with sewing and things, I'd love the luster china. And I'd like it as soon as I can have it. I'd like some cups and plates and a tea set with a thick, squatty pot. If you have to buy any of the china, I'll pay for it. A little bowl or so would be useful if you have one around.

I just came down this morning. The boat trip yesterday afternoon was very lovely. Sunny and cool and a brilliant, Mediterranean blue, as we came through all the islands and thoroughfares on the coast. I had a great vacation and I've gained many pounds.

Lots of love and be careful.

Virgil

但我觉得如果我们在家里都不坦诚，那么我们就什么也不是了。母亲一直有这样的想法，生孩子是有点粗俗的事情，好似上流社会的人不生孩子一样。然而实际上，"上流社会的人"恰恰是那些依然拥有 8 个或 10 个家庭成员的那些人，但如今的中等阶层却变得越来越自私和胆怯，要么根本不生孩子，要么全身心都放在一个被溺爱的孩子身上。我打赌罗伊会十分高兴的。

顺便说一句，你千万不要让家里人参与此事。保证每天要出去锻炼锻炼，到分娩时再去澄清，尽可能乘汽车去分娩。还有，请不要太节俭。我坚持认为你应该到医院去，最初的几个月由护士照顾。其他的任何方式都不安全。

请告诉家里人，他们真该好好地挨一顿揍，因为他们不想把此事告诉我（这真是令人忍无可忍），也因为他们对此事的态度既自私又愚蠢。

如果你不是太忙于缝纫或其他的事儿，我想要些彩瓷，并希望能尽快得到。我想要一些茶杯和盘子，还有一套茶具，里面配有厚厚的、圆圆的矮壶。如果你得去买这些瓷器，我会付钱的。如果你身边就有，一个小碗或其他什么也会对我有用的。

我今天早晨才下船。昨天下午的乘船旅行非常令人愉快。当我们游览所有的岛屿及海滨大道时，天空晴朗，气候凉爽，还有地中海那鲜艳夺目的蔚蓝。我度过了一个很棒的假期，而且我还长胖了许多。

献上无限的爱，请多珍重！

弗吉尔

1920 年 8 月 26 日

写于坎布里奇

# Benjamin Franklin to Miss Herbold
# 本杰明·富兰克林致赫伯德小姐

Philadelphia,

February 23, 1756.

I condole with you. We have lost a most dear and valuable relation. But it is the will of God and nature, that these mortal bodies be laid aside, when the soul is to enter into real life. This is rather an embryo state, a preparation for living.

A man is not completely born until he is dead. Why then should we grieve, that a new child is born among the immortals, a new member added to their happy society? We are spirits. That bodies should be lent us, while they can afford us pleasure, assist us in acquiring knowledge, or in doing good to our fellow creatures, is a kind and benevolent act of God. When they become unfit for these purposes, and afford us pain instead of pleasure, instead of an aid become an encumbrance, and answer none of the intentions for which they were given, it is equally kind and benevolent, that a way is provided by which we may get rid of them. Death is that way. We ourselves, in some cases, prudently choose a partial death. A mangled painful limb, which cannot be restored, we willingly cut off. He who plucks out a tooth, parts with it freely,

　　我要向你深表哀悼。我们失去了一位最亲爱可贵的亲人。但是这是上帝和自然的旨意，当灵魂进入天堂的时候，这些凡人的躯壳就要放置一边。这其实正是孕育状态，是生命的准备阶段。

　　一个人直到死的那一刻，才算得到真正的诞生。既然长生军里诞生了一个新婴儿，他们幸福的社会里又增加了一名新的成员，我们为什么还要为此感到悲伤呢？我们都是精灵。无比仁慈智慧的上帝行善施恩，赐予我们躯体，让我们享受快乐的生活；帮助我们获取知识，让我们造福于人类。当我们的躯体变得不再适应这些目的——不能提供给我们快乐，反而让我们痛苦；不能给我们帮助，反而成为我们的累赘；而且当它们无法完成上帝当初托付的使命时，同样恩惠仁慈的上帝提供了一种方式，让我们摆脱躯体。死亡就是那种方式。我们自己有时也会谨慎地选择一种局部的死亡。受伤疼痛的手脚，已经无法复原，我们会心甘情愿地把它切除。要拔牙的人，也会慷慨地舍弃它，因为拔掉之后痛苦就会随之而去。一个人如果完全脱离躯壳，就会立刻解脱掉一切痛苦以及

since the pain goes with it; and he, who quits the whole body, parts at once with all pains and possibilities of pains and diseases which it was liable to, or capable of making him suffer.

Our friend and we were invited abroad on a party of pleasure, which is to last forever. His chair was ready first, and he is gone before us. We could not all conveniently start together; and why should you and I be grieved at this, since we are soon to follow, and know where to find him?

Adieu.

B. Franklin

可能引起他痛苦和疾病的根源。

　　我们的朋友和我们自己早就受到邀请去参加一次欢乐的宴会,这是一场永不散席的宴会。他的座席早已准备好了,所以他会先我们一步而去。我们不能很方便地一同前往;既然不久之后我们就要随他而去,并且知道到哪里可以找到他,那你我又为什么要对此感到悲伤呢?

　　再见。

本·富兰克林

1756 年 2 月 23 日

写于费城

## *Abraham Lincoln to Johnston*
## 亚伯拉罕·林肯致约翰斯顿

(Dec. 24, 1848)

Dear Johnston:

Your request for eighty dollars, I do not think it best to comply with now. At the various times when I have helped you a little, you have said to me, "We can get along very well now," but in a very short time I find you in the same difficulty again. Now this can only happen by some defect in your conduct. What that defect is, I think I know. You are not lazy, and still you are an idler. I doubt whether since I saw you, you have done a good whole day's work, in any one day. You do not very much dislike to work, and still you do not work much, merely because it does not seem to you that you could get much for it.

This habit of uselessly wasting time, is the whole difficulty; it is vastly important to you, and still more so to your children, that you should break this habit. It is more important to them, because they have longer to live, and can keep out of an idle habit before they are in it, easier than they can get out after they are in.

You are now in need of some ready money; and what I propose is, that you shall go to work, "tooth and nail," for somebody who will give you money for it.

Let father and your boys take charge of your things at home—prepare

名人·小课堂

亚伯拉罕·林肯（Abraham Lincoln, 1809 ~ 1865 年）

美国政治家，第 16 任总统（任期：1861 年 3 月 4 日 ~ 1865 年 4 月 15 日），也是首位共和党籍总统。在任期间，他发表了《解放宣言》，领导人民进行了南北战争。林肯击败了南方分离势力，废除了奴隶制度，维护了国家的统一。但就在内战结束后不久，林肯不幸遇刺身亡。他是第一位遭到刺杀的美国总统，更是一位出身贫寒的伟大总统。

亲爱的约翰斯顿：

你向我借 80 美金，我觉得目前最好不要借给你。好几次我稍微帮助你之后，你跟我说"现在我们的生活可以过得非常好了"，但是过不了多久，我发现你又面临着同样的困境。现在，这种情况的发生只能说明，你自己的行为存在不足之处。是什么不足之处呢？我想我知道。你不懒，但却是个游手好闲的人。我怀疑自从上次看见你之后，你是否有认认真真工作过一天。你不太讨厌工作，但却不会拼命干活，唯一的原因是，你觉得你并不能从中获益多少。

所有的困难都缘于你那毫无益处的、浪费时间的恶习。改掉这个恶习对你来说非常重要，而对你的儿女则更加重要。这是因为他们的人生之路还很长，在没有养成散漫的习惯之前，尚可加以制止。这比养成之后再去改正要容易得多。

现在你需要些现钱；我建议你应该去工作，去为那个出钱给你的人

for a crop, and make the crop, and you go to work for the best money wages, or in discharge of any debt you owe, that you can get. And to secure you a fair reward for your labor, I now promise you that for every dollar you will, between this and the first of May, get for your own labor either in money or in your own indebtedness, I will then give you one other dollar.

By this, if you hire yourself at ten dollars a month, from me you will get ten more, making twenty dollars a month for your work. In this, I do not mean you shall go off to, or the lead mines, or the gold mines, in California, but I mean for you to go at it for the best wages you can get close to home—in Coles County.

Now if you will do this, you will soon be out of debt, and what is better, you will have a habit that will keep you from getting in debt again. But if I should now clear you out, next year you will be just as deep in as ever. You say you would almost give your place in Heaven for 70 or 80. Then you value your place in Heaven very cheaply, for I am sure you can with the offer I make you get the seventy or eighty dollars for four or five months' work. You say if I furnish you the money you will deed me the land, and if you don't pay the money back, you will deliver possession —Nonsense! If you can't now live with the land, how will you then live without it? You have always been kind to me, and I do not now mean to be unkind to you. On the contrary, if you will but follow my advice, you will find it worth more than eight times eighty dollars to you.

Affectionately

Your brother

"拼命地"工作。

让你爸爸和你的儿子们去负责家里的事——为春播和秋收做好准备，你自己去做些最挣钱的工作，或者用你所得的工资抵债。为了使你的劳动获得好的回报，我现在答应你，从今天到 5 月 1 号，只要你工作挣到 1 块钱或是偿还了 1 块钱的债，我就另外再给你 1 块钱。

这样的话，如果你每月挣 10 块钱，你可以从我这儿再多得 10 块钱，那么你一个月就能挣 20 块钱。我不是说让你到加利福尼亚州的铅矿或金矿去，而是让你在离家近的地方找个最挣钱的工作——就在柯尔斯县境内。

如果你现在愿意这样做，你很快就能还清债务。更好的是，你会养成远离债务的好习惯。但是，如果我现在帮你还了债，明年你又会像以前一样负债累累。你说，你愿意用你在天堂的席位去换取七八十块钱。那样的话，你就把你在天堂的席位看得太廉价了。因为我保证照我说的去做，你工作四五个月就能挣到那七八十块钱。你又说，如果我借给你钱，你愿意把田产抵押给我；若是将来你还不清钱，那田地就归我所有——胡说八道！假如现在你有田地都无法生存，将来没有田地又怎么存活呢？你一向对我很好，我现在也不是对你无情无义。相反，如果你肯采纳我的建议，你会发现，对你来说，这比 80 块钱 8 倍还值得多！

挚爱你的哥哥

亚·林肯

1848 年 12 月 24 日

For my brothers Carl and (Johann) Beethoven,

O ye men, who think or say that I am malevolent, stubborn, or misanthropic, how greatly do ye wrong me, you do not know the secret causes of my seeming, from childhood my heart and mind were disposed to the gentle feeling of good will, I was even ever eager to accomplish great deeds, but reflect now that for 6 years I have been in a hopeless case, aggravated by senseless physicians, cheated year after year in the hope of improvement, finally compelled to face the prospect of a lasting malady (whose cure will take years, or, perhaps, be impossible), born with an ardent and lively temperament, even susceptible to the diversions of society, I was compelled early to isolate myself, to live in loneliness, when I at times tried to forget all this, O'how harshly was I repulsed by the doubly sad experience of my bad hearing, and yet it was impossible for me to say to men speak louder, shout, for I am deaf.

Ah how could I possibly admit an infirmity in the one sense which should have been more perfect in me than in others, a sense which I once possessed in highest perfection, a perfection such as few surely in my profession enjoy or ever have enjoyed. —O I cannot do it, therefore forgive me when you see

给我的兄弟卡尔和（约翰）贝多芬：

啊，兄弟们，你们说我心肠不好、固执或者厌世，你们多么冤枉我啊！你们不知道引起我表面这些特点的真正原因。从小，我的内心就倾向于正面看待事物，我甚至曾渴望将来做一番大事业。但是现在回想一下，6 年以来我一直处于一种无望之中，而这种无望的感觉又拜那些庸医所赐日益加剧，他们年复一年地欺骗我有治愈的希望，可最后却不得不面对终身残疾的命运（这种病需要很多年才能治好，或者，可能根本就治不好）。我生来性情热忱活泼，甚至喜欢社交，但现在年纪轻轻就被迫离群索居，过着孤独寂寞的生活。有时，我试图忘记这一切，但是我却被听力不好而带来的双重的悲惨经历所击退。这是多么残酷的事啊！我不可能去跟其他人说"大声点，使劲嚷，我耳朵聋"。

我怎么可能公开承认我的耳朵有问题呢？我的听觉一直比别人好——以前非常灵敏，同行中很少有人能和我比——哦，我真的做不到。当你们看到我躲开你们时（其实我非常想和你们在一起），请你们原谅我。我的不幸令我感到加倍的痛苦，因为它必然会引起别人对我的误解。对

me draw back when I would gladly mingle with you, my misfortune is doubly painful because it must lead to my being misunderstood, for me there can be no recreation in society of my fellows, refined intercourse, mutual exchange of thought, only just as little as the greatest needs command may I mix with society.

I must live like an exile, if I approach near to people a hot terror seizes upon me, a fear that I may be subjected to the danger of letting my condition be observed—thus it has been during the last half year which I spent in the country, commanded by my intelligent physician to spare my hearing as much as possible, in this almost meeting my present natural disposition, although I sometimes ran counter to it, yielding to my inclination for society, but what a humiliation when one stood beside me and heard a flute in the distance and I heard nothing, or someone heard the shepherd singing and again I heard nothing, such incidents brought me to the verge of despair, but little more and I would have put an end to my life—only art it was that withheld me, ah it seemed impossible to leave the world until I had produced all that I felt called upon to produce, and so I endured this wretched existence—truly wretched, and excitable body which a sudden change can throw from the best into the worst state—Patience—it is said I must now choose for my guide, I have done so, I hope my determination will remain firm to endure until it pleases the inexorable Parcae to break the thread, perhaps I shall get better, perhaps not, I am prepared.

...

To you brother Carl I give special thanks for the attachment you have displayed toward me of late. It is my wish that your lives may be better and

我而言，再也不能和我的伙伴们一起娱乐、精确交谈、互换思想了。除非万不得已，我总是尽量避免和社会接触。

　　我必须像个流亡者一样地活着，假如我与别人走得靠近时，巨大的恐惧就会笼罩着我，我担心自己的情况可能会被别人发现——这半年来一直是如此。在乡下的这些日子里，我是完全按照医生的嘱咐，尽可能多地让我的听觉得到休息，这也完全符合我目前的禀性。尽管，我有时会与之背道而驰，屈服于自己对社会的向往。可是，每当身边的人听见远处的笛声，而我却什么也听不见，或有人听见牧人歌唱，而我还是什么也听不见，这是多么大的一种耻辱啊！这些事情把我推到了绝望的边缘，但是若再多一点点这样的事情，我将会结束自己的生命——但是艺术制止了我。在我还没有把自己认为必须创作出来的作品全部创作完毕之前，我似乎是不可能离开人间的！于是，我忍受着这种痛苦的生活。真是痛苦极了，我的身体容易激动，只要突然有一点变化，就会从最好变成最坏。忍耐，人们说我现在应该把它当作指南，我已经这样做了，并且我希望自己忍耐的决心能长久保持下去，直到无情的命运女神宣布我生命的终结。也许我的病会慢慢变好，也许不会，对此我已有心理准备。

　　……

　　卡尔弟弟，我非常感激你最近对我的深情。我祝愿你们的生活过得比我更好，拥有的烦恼比我更少。你们要用美德教育儿女，因为只有美德能给人带来幸福，而不是金钱——这是我的经验之谈。在不幸中，支

freer from care than I have had, recommend virtue to your children, it alone can give happiness, not money, I speak from experience, it was virtue that upheld me in misery, to it next to my art I owe the fact that I did not end my life by suicide.

Farewell and love each other—I thank all my friends, particularly Prince Lichnowsky and Professor Schmid—I desire that the instruments from Prince L. be preserved by one of you but let no quarrel result from this, so soon as they can serve you a better purpose sell them, how glad will I be if I can still be helpful to you in my grave—with joy I hasten toward death—if it comes before I shall have had an opportunity to show all my artistic capacities it will still come too early for me despite my hard fate and I shall probably wish that it had come later—but even then I am satisfied, will it not free me from a state of endless suffering? Come when thou will I shall meet thee bravely, Farewell and do not wholly forget me when I am dead. I deserve this of you in having often in life thought of you, how to make you happy, be so—

Heiglnstadt,

October 6th, 1802

Ludwig van Beethoven

持我的就是美德。我之所以没有通过自杀结束自己的生命，除了为了我的艺术外，其次就应归功于美德。

再见了，愿你们彼此相爱——感谢我所有的朋友，尤其是李赫诺斯基亲王和许密特教授。我希望你们二人中有一个人能替我保存李赫诺斯基亲王送给我的那些乐器，但不要为此引起争执。一旦这些东西对你们有更大的用途时，你们可以把它们卖掉。如果我死后还能对你们有所帮助，我将感到多么高兴啊！我微笑面对日益趋近的死神，但如果死神在我还未有机会展示我的全部艺术才能之前到来的话，我觉得还是来得太早了些。尽管我的命运坎坷，我可能还是会希望那一天晚些到来。不过，即使那样，我也会心满意足的。那样不就能把我从无穷无尽的苦难中解脱出来吗？你们愿意来的什么时候就来吧，我会鼓起勇气见你们的。再见了，我死后不要把我完全地忘了。我值得你们的纪念，因为我在世的时候经常想念你们，并想着如何使你们快乐。但愿……

路德维希·凡·贝多芬

1802 年 10 月 6 日

写于海格伦斯塔特

## *Theodore Roosevelt to Ted*
## 西奥多·罗斯福致泰德

Oyster Bay,

May 7th, 1901.

Blessed Ted,

It was the greatest fun seeing you, and I really had a satisfactory time with you, and came away feeling that you were doing well. I am entirely satisfied with your standing, both in your studies and in athletics. I want you to do well in your sports, and I want even more to have you do well with your books but I do not expect you to stand first in either, if so to stand could cause you overwork and hurt your health. I always believe in going hard at everything, whether it is Latin or mathematics, boxing or football, but at the same time I want to keep the sense of proportion. It is never worthwhile to absolutely exhaust one's self or to take big chances unless for an adequate object. I want you to keep in training the faculties, which would make you, if the need arose, able to put your last ounce of pluck and strength into a contest. But I do not want you to squander these qualities. To have you play football as well as you do, and make a good name in boxing and wrestling, and be cox of your second crew, and stand second or third in your class in the studies, is all right. I should

**名人小课堂**

西奥多·罗斯福（Theodore Roosevelt, Jr., 1858～1919年）

人称老罗斯福，美国军事家、政治家，第26任总统（1901～1909）。他出生于纽约市一个荷兰家庭，毕业于哈佛大学，他热衷于政治运动。1901年总统威廉·麦金莱（William McKinley）遇刺身亡，他继任成为美国总统，时年42岁。罗斯福为人正直，力求公正。他的独特个性和改革主义政策，使他成为美国历史上最伟大的总统之一。

亲爱的泰德：

见到你我真的非常高兴，与你一起，我真的度过了一段愉快的时光。离开时，我觉得你干得很不错。我非常满意你在学习和体育方面所取得的名次。我希望你在体育方面做得好，更希望你在读书方面也做得好。但是，如果得第一名需要你过度用功，进而损害到你的健康的话，我不期望你在任何一方面名列第一。我一直坚信，做任何事，都要全力以赴，无论是学拉丁文还是数学，练拳击还是足球，但同时也要保持均衡。除非为了适当的目标，要不绝不值得把人弄得精疲力竭或去冒巨大风险。我要你继续训练本领，一旦需要，就可以将你的全部勇气和力量投入竞争。但我不想你滥用这些本领。你要尽量打好足球，在拳击和摔跤方面取得一个好名次，成为二线队员的领袖人物，而且学习方面要在班上排到二三名，做到这些就行了。如果看到你在班上的名次降到中等水平，那我将很伤心，因为那样的话，你就要到19岁才能上大学，进而要迟

be rather sorry to see you drop too near the middle of your class, because, as you cannot enter college until you are nineteen, and will therefore be a year later in entering life. I want you to be prepared in the best possible way, so as to make up for the delay. But I know that all you can do you will do to keep substantially the position in the class that you have so far kept, and I have entire trust in you, for you have always deserved it.

一年步入社会。我要你尽可能地作好充分准备，以便弥补这种耽搁。但我知道，你所能做的一切就是要大体上保持住目前你在班上所处的位置。我完全相信你，因为你总是值得信任。

1901 年 5 月 7 日

写于牡蛎湾

*let's white that letter we thought of writing*
*"one of these days",*
曾"打算有那么一天"去写的信，
就在今天写吧